In Service to Their Country

Praise for *In Service to Their Country*

"This is an inspiring book that illuminates the influence of education in our lives. The students of Christchurch School received much more than education over the course of the years they attended; they received inspiration and a sense of the importance of national service and sacrifice for something greater than themselves. Captain Monroe's effort highlights his alma mater's contributions to our nation's history in the lives and actions of its students. In this flowing account, which spans more than a century, it becomes clear that they were given more than a diploma, they were given a sense of vocation."

—Captain Henry J. "Jerry" Hendrix, USN, Director of Naval History

"This unusual, interesting book focuses on the preparation for military life that can come from private secondary school culture. By using testimony of veterans who graduated from Christchurch School, above the banks of the Rappahannock River, author/editor Alexander 'Sandy' Monroe shows the common threads that link these two ways of life. These men and women, who range back from World War II to the recent wars in the Middle East, recall their adaptation to the values, discipline, and structure taught by Christchurch's dedicated headmasters and staff, and they recall how this culture enabled them to adapt to similar values practiced in the military. They excelled as leaders who had assimilated the concepts of honor, integrity, and discipline by the time they graduated. This small school on the banks of Virginia's lovely Rappahannock River has provided more than 325 men and women to the uniformed services of the United States, perhaps more than its fair share. This story will have resonance for its similarity to the hundreds of other preparatory schools whose students have done their duty for God and Country."

—William S. Dudley, Director of Naval History, 1995–2004

"Ironically, one of the outstanding graduates of Christchurch School that Captain 'Sandy' Monroe failed to document was himself! A naval officer with decades of service, Monroe, in his efforts on behalf of the Naval History and Heritage Command, has been instrumental in assuring that hundreds of stories of American sailors serving at home and abroad have been preserved for future generations. With his background as a Christchurch School alumnus and as a chronicler of history, a book has been produced detailing the tales of just *some* of that school's graduates who went on to serve in the Army, Navy, Marine Corps, Air Force and Coast Guard. *In Service to Their Country* is a series of stories in which those in the Rappahannock River area—indeed in all of Virginia—can take great pride."

—Commander David F. Winkler, USN (Retired), historian at the Naval Historical Foundation and author of *Amirs, Admirals and Desert Sailor: Bahrain, the U.S. Navy and the Arabian Gulf.*

In Service to Their Country

Christchurch School and the American Uniformed Services

By Captain Alexander "Sandy" G. Monroe
Captain, United States Navy (Ret.)

PLEASANT LIVING
BOOKS

ISBN 978-0-615-91429-9

Library of Congress Control Number: 2013919966

Front cover photo credit: American troops going through the smoky ruins of Messina, Sicily, 16 August 1943. National Archives Photo.

Back cover photo credit: U.S. Navy photo of the USS *Lewis B. Puller* (FFG-23). Supplied courtesy of the Defense Visual Information Center.

Published by

PLEASANT LIVING
BOOKS

www.pleasantlivingmagazine.com/books

For my parents, who made Christchurch possible,
my stepmother, Louise Robertson Monroe, MD,
and my late wife, Elizabeth Ambler Monroe (1941–2011)

Speech to the Nation, May 19, 1940
Winston S. Churchill, Prime Minister, United Kingdom

Today is Trinity Sunday. Centuries ago words were written to be a call and spur to faithful servants of Truth and Justice: Arm yourselves and be ye men of valor and in readiness for the conflict . . . for it is better for us to perish in battle than look upon the outrage of our nation and altar. As the Will of God is in heaven, even so let it be . . .

(Churchill quoting from 1 Maccabees 3:58–60)

Table of Contents

List of Illustrations

FOREWORD

It is now nearly ninety-two years since the first students entered Christchurch School. It has come a long way since those first boys arrived at the school, which was located in the "white house," the first school building on the tract of land known as the Eastman Farm, which overlooks the Rappahannock from a hillside in Middlesex County.

Back then, the school was, in the words of an early catalog, "the only country school for boys on Virginia's salt water." It was to produce individuals of "high character, pure and healthy bodies, well furnished minds and a spirit of unselfish service." In later years, it was described as a place where young men might be sent to remove them from the "distractions of the modern city." The focus was on providing solid academic preparation so that graduates could pursue and complete the standard four-year college programs in the normal amount of time. Some of the students came from weak academic backgrounds and the curriculum was indeed daunting. Many students thrived in the environment and went on to successful careers in a variety of fields.

The years since Christchurch's founding have brought their share of challenges and opportunities. Today the school has 204 students from fourteen states and nine foreign countries and is entering a new and exciting phase in its life by providing a coeducational academic program for its boarding students.

In the years since its founding, many alumni faculty and staff have served in the uniformed services of the United States in a variety of ways. Some have served with conspicuous gallantry in combat while others have served in non-combatant roles of equal importance to the defense of our nation.

Captain Alexander G. "Sandy" Monroe, U.S. Navy (Ret.), class of 1960, who has been decorated for exemplary service to the government in the area of naval history, has in this book given us an account of their military service and the preparation provided for it by the school, skillfully fashioning a story told by members of the Christchurch family in their own words. In some cases, portions of their stories are taken from never-before-published public records and photographs.

I commend this book to all who share a love for Christchurch School and hold special memories of their time spent on that hillside overlooking the Rappahannock River in Middlesex County.

John W. Craine, Jr., '64
Vice Admiral, USN (Ret.)

Preface

A few years ago, a group of Christchurch alumni, all of whom had served in the uniformed services of the United States, teamed up to install a monument honoring all "Faculty, Alumni and Staff" who had so served since the beginning of the school. The term "uniformed" services was chosen for the inscription because it was possible that some had served in the Coast and Geodetic Survey, also known as the National Oceanographic and Atmospheric Administration Corps, or the United States Public Health Service, whose members have rendered distinguished service often in combat. The logical extension of erection of the monument was writing a book about those who have served.

Complete records of the military service of those memorialized on the monument did not exist. The first task, therefore, was to develop an accurate list, a job that goes on to this very day. Over 345 names have been gathered, and there are probably many more to be added. It is the hope of all who have gathered them thus far that more will emerge and be added to the list on the school website. The next task was to research the relevant records of the services and those "alumni" groups of veterans' organizations to learn more. That arduous task led from the Naval History and Heritage Command to the Army's Center for Military History, to the Air Force Historical Office at Bolling Air Force Base in Washington to the National Archives. It has led to long-forgotten ships' deck logs and copies of submarine patrol reports, missing aircrew reports and other primary and secondary material. It is a rich, often deeply moving vein, and where appropriate sources have been noted.

In fashioning this volume, there has been no intention to slight those in the Christchurch family who, for reasons beyond their control, in some cases injuries sustained in athletics at Christchurch, were unable to serve. In some cases oral histories have been edited because of space considerations, but the meaning and intent of the subject has not been compromised. The objective was to give human form and substance to the simple granite monument that overlooks the constantly flowing Rappahannock River. It frequently shimmers azure blue under a brilliant sun, but can become leaden grey in chilling stormy times.

The result of the research and tabulation is now before you, so that in the words of Saint Paul, you may "read, mark and inwardly digest, holding fast to that which is good . . ." It has been an honor to carry out this task, which is being completed in a glorious place overlooking the silent river that has been a source of strength to so many in years past and will be in the times ahead. I have been greatly assisted by a number of individuals but any errors of fact or interpretation are mine alone.

Alexander G. Monroe
Captain, USN (Ret.)
Spring, 2012
at Weems, Virginia

Acknowledgments

This book could not have been written without the help of many people, in the Christchurch family and beyond, and I wish to thank them.

I am most grateful to those who have done oral histories, whose names are in the table of contents. Further, I wish to recognize those who have provided insights and frequently copies of original documents that give some flavor to the work. They are: T. Freeland Mason '41; William Ray Winder '42; V. Randolph "Dolph" Chowning '42; William G. Broaddus '61; C. Nelson Williams IV '61; and Thomas S. Marchant, Jr.

I thank M. Huntley Galleher, Associate Director of Development, and Patty Rimbey and Rebecca Hogge of his office, who have responded to my many requests with skill, marked patience and, in the patois of Bob Yarbrough, "alacrity." I appreciate the responsiveness of Mr. Scott Blankenship in providing photographs.

I have benefitted greatly from the critical reading of the work as it progressed and the cogent suggestions of former Dean Robert C. Goodman and his wife Jinny; Somerville "Spud" Parker; Gerry Cooper '53; Breckinridge Montague '66; Clayton Wagner; Patrice Van Swall; Margaret Peters; Frances W. Twiss; Sue Lane Winstead; Bruce Wilson; Captain William R. McClintock, U.S. Navy (Ret.); Kathleen P. Decker, M.D.; Captain Calvin Tanck, U.S. Navy; Vice Admiral John W. Craine, Jr., '64, U.S. Navy (Ret.); and Captain John P. Cann III, U.S. Navy (Ret.). These suggestions and, in some cases, changes in the text have strengthened the end result considerably.

I am grateful for the splendid support that has been provided by Dr. Timothy Francis, who takes justifiable pride in being a Chief Intelligence Specialist in the U.S. Navy; Dr. Regina Akers and Timothy Frank of the Naval History and Heritage Command at the Washington Navy Yard; Yeoman First Class Omara Boulware, U.S. Navy, of Naval History Detachment Two Zero Six; Mary Laura Kludy of the Archivist's Office of the Preston Library at Virginia Military Institute; Kara Newcomer of the Marine Corps History Division at Quantico, Virginia; and staff at the American Military Cemeteries at Colleville Sur Mer, France, and Henri Chappelle, Belgium.

I appreciate permission to quote from the works of William Styron provided by his widow, Rose, and by James L. W. West III, his biographer, and permission to use portions of an article in the U.S. Naval Institute Proceedings granted by Admiral James G. Stavridis, U.S. Navy, Supreme Allied Commander Europe. I also thank Colonel Gregory Julian, U.S. Army, formerly of the staff of Supreme Allied Commander Europe, now on the staff of the Commander, United States Southern Command, for his assistance. Finally, I am very grateful for the splendid editorial work of Annie Tobey of Brandylane Publishers. She has, tactfully and skillfully, provided focus and clarity where it was earlier missing.

INTRODUCTION

In its summer 1995 issue, *Christchurch Magazine* ran a photograph, taken in the fall of 1988, of two U.S. Navy captains: Alexander G. Monroe '60 and John W. Craine, Jr., '64.

Between them the photograph shows the skylight from the steam sloop USS *Hartford*, Admiral David Farragut's flagship at the Battle of Mobile Bay. These two graduates had met fortuitously in the Washington Navy Yard after Sandy returned from the Arabian Gulf. He had carried out a special assignment for the Director of Naval History in connection with Operation Earnest Will, the re-flagging of supertankers undertaken by President Reagan so that the flow of Gulf oil would not be interrupted. Johnny Craine '64[1] a naval aviator who had flown numerous missions over North Vietnam and later became a vice admiral, was as a captain the Navy's special assistant for Flag Matters, the officer initially responsible for recommending to the Chief of Naval Personnel the duty assignments of Navy admirals. They were but two of a number of alumni who have served in the uniformed services of the United States in the time since the school was founded in 1921. The long line of those in the Christchurch family who have served has been memorialized by a simple granite monument that overlooks the Rappahannock River. The new natural sciences building named for him honors 1st Lieutenant Lewis B. Puller, Jr., '63, USMC, who served with great intrepidity and was maimed in the Vietnam War in 1968. He later won a Pulitzer Prize for his biography, *Fortunate Son*. Tragically, he took his own life many years later and rests in Arlington National Cemetery.

This photo stimulated an effort to collect data and oral histories of Christchurch alumni who have served in the uniformed services of the United States. What are those characteristics, factors and influences common to the Christchurch experience and serving in the armed forces? How are the experiences related, if at all? How are personalities of those in charge at school and those in the service similar? Where, for example, in the service might one find a William Smith, Branch Spalding, Emmet Hoy, Bob Yarbrough, Hatcher Williams, Somerville Parker, Bob Goodman, Gerry Cooper, Grover Jones, Bill Davies, Fred Riley, "Rock" Poulson or Bob Phipps? Some of those whose oral

Captains Alexander G. Monroe '60, USN, and John W. Craine, Jr., '64, USN, at the Naval History and Heritage Command in November 1988 (Collections of the Naval History and Heritage Command

First Lieutenant Lewis B. Puller, Jr., '63, USMC, at Marine Corps Base, Quantico, Virginia, 1968 (Official U.S. Marine Corps Photograph, A557562)

histories appear hereafter served full careers while others served for relatively short periods and then returned to civilian life and pursued productive careers in medicine, law and public service. Christchurch alumni have served in war and peacetime in the Aleutians, the hedgerows of Normandy, the Ardennes Forest, the air over Nazi- occupied France and Germany, aboard ships invading Japanese-held islands, garrisons, air stations and shipyards in the United States, Vietnam, the Arabian Gulf area and on and on. This volume relates the contributions of those who cannot speak for themselves, as well as those who can. The search, sometimes sad, has been far reaching and rewarding. The compilation shows that there is much in common between the values and standards inculcated at Christchurch and those expected in all the armed forces in which members of the Christchurch family have served.

What is distinctive about Christchurch and other private secondary schools nationwide is that they seek to educate and train students for taking responsibility for their actions and exercising leadership. This has been demonstrated repeatedly in academic achievements, in later service in the armed forces and in subsequent vocational pursuits, whether civilian or military. In the armed forces, members are trained to accept responsibility. One need only consider the lives and careers of such individuals as Presidents John F. Kennedy, George H. W. Bush, George W. Bush, Senators Claiborne Pell and John McCain and astronauts Mike Collins and Pete Conrad.[2] The achievements of John Kennedy in the Navy and after are well known, as are those of George H. W. Bush, whose service as the youngest naval aviator was a prelude to a successful career in business and government service. Clearly a sense of duty and personal integrity, hallmarks of successful figures in any calling and qualities stressed at Christchurch and places like it, motivated John McCain, a graduate of Episcopal High School, in his travail as a prisoner of war.

The first challenges in the post-World War II era resulted from Russian expansion and the abrupt dropping of what Prime Minister Winston Churchill of Great Britain called an "Iron Curtain" over captive eastern European states. Even before the conclusion of the war, features of the Cold War emerged. For example, Bob Mumper '42 was shot down in the waning days of World War II in Europe. He and other American aviators were held in a POW camp in Barth, at the edge of the Baltic Sea, an area to become part of the Russian zone of divided post-war Germany. Here he became sick from tainted food. Russians initially denied the other allied powers the right to fly aircraft into the area to repatriate prisoners, and only intercession by the supreme commander of the Allied Expeditionary Force made the evacuation—known as Operation Revival and conducted from May 13 through May 15, 1945—possible.

The ensuing Cold War, referred to as a "long twilight struggle" by President

John F. Kennedy in his inaugural address in 1961, was a period of nearly continuous evasive hostility that ended with demolition of the Berlin Wall in 1989. Christchurch alumni served in this period and in the stalemate in Vietnam, and continue to do so in today's operations in the Arabian Gulf, Afghanistan and the Caribbean. The Cold War has given way to a "War on Terror," which is, if anything, more dangerous and challenging. As the attacks of September 11, 2001, illustrate, the country can no longer take advantage of an oceanic barrier. Rather, United States Armed Forces must rely on non-doctrinal methods such as giving medical care to indigenous populations and building schools. Specific challenges have changed, as have operational methods, but Christchurch alumni continue in the tradition of service to the country. John Craine '64 opined that the common element, to his thinking, was that both at Christchurch and in the Navy, "You are judged not by who you are but what you are." This is, of course, true; but as we explore the recollections of those who follow, it may well be that other common elements will become clear.

War Comes to Christchurch

William Styron '42, author of *Sophie's Choice*, gave the commencement address at Christchurch in 1975. Styron, who had served as a Marine in World War II and was recalled to active duty in the Korean War, remembered being in study hall on December 8, 1941, the day after the Japanese surprise attack on Pearl Harbor. He said:

> As we sat in study hall listening to the radio and President Roosevelt's call for a declaration of war against the Axis powers— few of us could realize how irrevocably things would be changed— for us and the world and how all of our lives thenceforth would be in one way or another determined by the existence of war.[3]

December 7, 1941, some twenty years after the founding of Christchurch, was the capstone of a period of gathering hostility that began in earnest on October 15, 1938, when German forces marched unopposed into the Sudetenland, an event that was not, as Neville Chamberlain earlier said after the Munich Conference, "peace in our time." This was followed barely one month later by the terrible initiation of hostilities against Jews known as Kristallnacht, in which the windows and storefronts of Jewish shopkeepers and merchants all over Germany were shattered and the contents looted. In rapid succession, Hitler unleashed his forces against Poland, overran the Low Countries and conquered Norway and Denmark. By the summer of 1940, France was driven under the Nazi heel and England stood alone. The British Expeditionary Force (BEF), or what remained of it, had been hastily evacuated from Dunkirk. British Prime Minister Winston Churchill predicted in June 1940 that "very soon the whole might and fury of Nazi Germany would be turned against the United Kingdom for Hitler knows that he must break us in this island or lose the war . . ."[4]

From the fall of France in June 1940 until the Japanese attack on Pearl Harbor, President Roosevelt led the United States on a path fraught with danger. While there was widespread feeling that "something should be done" to assist the British, there was widespread disagreement about what exactly should be done and how much of it should be done. In September 1940, just prior to national elections, in a controversial act, Roosevelt loaned fifty overage destroyers to the British in exchange for basing rights in Canada, Bermuda and the Caribbean, responding to Churchill's impassioned cry for help.[5] The Republican candidate for president, Wendell Willkie, criticized the president for not seeking congressional approval of the deal. It was thought by some that the United States would be immune from attack because of the oceanic isolation of Europe from the western hemisphere.

Editorial cartoon by Fred O. Seibel in the September 5, 1940,
(Courtesy *Richmond Times-Dispatch*)

Quickly, a sharply divided Congress enacted the first peacetime conscription act and, by March 1941, created the Lend Lease Act, which enabled Roosevelt to "lend" vast quantities of war material rather than requiring "cash and carry" purchase as had previously been required. The debates surrounding the passage of the Burke-Wadsworth Act establishing the draft were so contentious that it was reported that two House members engaged in fisticuffs, and the bill passed. Since the initial term of conscription was for only one year, extension had to be approved separately, and its extension a year later was approved in the House of Representatives by only one vote! Earlier, in September 1939, the American government had established a Neutrality Patrol. After negotiation of the ABC Agreement of March 27, 1941, United States naval aviators flew in British patrol aircraft in highly sensitive, classified operations. In fact, on May 26, 1941, the battleship *Bismarck*, later to be sunk by the Royal Navy, was sighted through a break in the overcast skies by Ensign Leonard B. Smith, U.S. Navy, an officer on an exchange tour flying in a British Catalina, based at Royal Air Force Squadron 209, Lough Erne, Northern Ireland.[6]

While attempting to move gingerly, American naval forces were resolute, and—concurrent with German U-boat attacks on the USS *Kearney* (DD-432) on October 17, 1941, and the USS *Reuben James* (DD-245), which was sunk with 115 of her crew in the cold waters west of Iceland barely two weeks later—operated with "shoot to kill" orders. Later, on November 6, 1941, the cruiser USS *Omaha* (CL-4) and destroyer USS *Somers* (DD-381) intercepted and seized the German blockade runner MS *Odenwald*, which had been disguised as the American merchant ship SS *Willmoto*[7]. The expectation was that war with Germany was inevitable. The months before December 7, 1941, were a terrible period of undeclared war, and by the time the class of 1942 graduated, the United States and its allies were fighting for survival in the war against the Axis powers. Corregidor, a tadpole-shaped island in Manila Bay commonly known as "the Rock," had been surrendered on May 6, 1942, after four months of siege. Earlier, on February 4, 1942, the USS *Trout* (SS-202) removed some twenty tons of gold bullion and silver pesos, the reserves of Philippine banks, and transferred it to Hawaii. Slightly more than a month later, in the dusk of March 11, 1942, the Commander of U.S. Forces Far East, General Douglas MacArthur, and his family left by PT boat. Lieutenant John D. Bulkeley, USN, and the crew of USS *PT-41* travelled over six hundred miles through enemy-infested waters, with no radar and unreliable navigational aids, and left the general and his family on Mindanao, where they were taken to Australia in a B-17. Some nurses were later evacuated from the Rock by a Navy PBY Catalina and the submarine USS *Spearfish* (SS-190),[8] but most of its brave defenders were marched off through the streets of Manila to former jails that were converted into POW camps. The allies had not yet achieved success at Midway and Guadalcanal.

Many of the students gathered in study hall on that Monday morning in 1941 would depart to serve in the Armed Forces, and those who went before them also served. William Robards '27 commanded USS *O'Reilly* (DE-330), which made repeated convoys to Algeria and Great Britain, later sailed to the Pacific and was decommissioned in 1946. Miles Libbey, Jr., '35, a 1940 Naval

Academy graduate who would later play a key role under Admiral Hyman G. Rickover in the development of the nuclear submarine USS *Nautilus* (SSN-571), was assigned to the heavy cruiser USS *Wichita* (CA-45). In late April 1942, the ship participated in operations covering convoys PQ 11 and 15 to Murmansk in the Soviet Union, and fired on a German Condor reconnaissance aircraft in the Denmark Strait. Later it participated in Operation Torch, the November 1942 invasion of North Africa involving an exchange of shellfire with the Vichy French battleship *Jean Bart* and shore batteries at Casablanca, Morocco. During that exchange, the ship was struck by shellfire, which injured fourteen sailors. In the 1943 invasion of Attu and Kiska in the Aleutian Islands, the ship prepared the landing grounds with heavy naval bombardment. Malcus Horton '39 joined the Royal Canadian Air Force, later transferred to the Army Air Corps and ultimately retired from the U.S. Air Force as a colonel after a full career.

Freeland Mason '41 recalled that Headmaster William Smith, who was held in high esteem by the vast majority of students, observed that "true soldiers were dedicated and disciplined," and that he kept the students who were still in school informed of the progress of the war at daily morning assemblies. Ray Winder '42 noted that "our football coach was summarily fired for being a Nazi sympathizer." As masters enlisted in the services, "older retired teachers such as 'Pop' Wylie were hired. The impact of the war was always at hand, and gas, food, tires and other items were rationed . . ."[9]

Robert Holloway '40 was killed on September 5, 1943, in a cross-country training flight in Lake Cormorant, Mississippi, while in Army Air Force flight school at Hobbs Field, New Mexico.[10] Robert Mumper '42 of Hagerstown, Maryland, along with his classmate Randy "Dolph" Chowning of Lancaster County, Virginia, joined the Army Air Force. William "Mick" Bowman '42 of New York City, mentioned in the 1975 Christchurch commencement address as a source of illicit beer by his friend Bill Styron '42, joined the Army Ground Forces, serving first in the Signal Corps. Byrd Holloway '42, who survived the war, was drafted partway through his first year at Hampden-Sydney College and served in the Pacific, first in glider operations of the 11th Airborne Division and then as a paratrooper. Frank B. Tavenner '42 landed in Normandy and fought across Europe, enduring the storms and combat of the Battle of the Bulge along with his classmate, James S. G. Davenport, who was known as "Port." Bob Mumper, a radio operator in a B-17 nicknamed "In Like Errol," bailed out as the doomed aircraft—one of 2,300 mounted in a major March 30, 1945, air strike to cripple whatever remained of the German Navy's submarine pens in the Wilhelmshaven/Bremen complex[11]—was hit, and he and a fellow crewman were thrown to the aircraft's overhead. Only with the assistance of his comrade, Sergeant Chuck Majors, was he able to don another parachute and thus bail out.[12] He landed in the backyard of a housewife who was hanging her wash out to dry in a residential suburb of Hamburg. Surrounded by hostile German civilians, he was marched off to spend the remainder of the war in Stalag Luft One, a German POW camp at the edge of the Baltic Sea.[13]

United States Army Air Force aircraft number, 42-102590, "In Like Errol" (Courtesy 91st Heavy Bombardment Group Association)

William "Mick" Bowman was severely wounded and frostbitten in the Battle of the Bulge, Hitler's final spasmodic Christmas 1944 attempt to avoid inevitable defeat by the Allies. Later, Ray Winder '42, who served as a pilot-trainee and later as a waist gunner, recalled while sailing with his friend in the school's sturdy Hampton Ones the ineffable yet strangely healing powers of the Rappahannock. Mick, wounded by German 88 shrapnel on February 10, 1945, in the aftermath of the Battle of the Bulge, had gone without prompt medical care and awoke to find chaplains "saying the words" over him and doctors trying to determine whether they should amputate his leg. As Winder noted in a letter to Bowman's children after his 1997 funeral at the Christ Church[14] burial ground just down the road from school, he was appalled to find his friend in the state he was after being brought back to the United States to continue his recovery. Far from being the ebullient Mick Bowman he remembered from their student days, the wounded soldier was "a walking dead man with no energy, no animation, no smile . . ." Gradually, as they sailed during that furlough period, he saw his friend's color return, and his strength was augmented, as if by an almost spiritual infusion. "The Mick was going to be ok . . . well ok if you forgot about the pain that never left him, whenever the weather got cool because of the frostbite he suffered in that hellish winter at the Battle of the Bulge."

Before September 2, 1945, when Foreign Minister Shigemitsu and his underlings clambered up the gangway to the quarterdeck of the USS *Missouri* (BB-63), anchored in Tokyo Bay in sight of Mount Fujiyama, to surrender on behalf of the Emperor of Japan, six Christchurch alumni had lost their lives in the conflict. They are Charles L. Darbie '26, of the U.S. Army, Richie N. Henderson '35 of the U.S. Navy, Robert G. Holloway '40 of the U.S. Army Air Force, together with Sydney A. Vincent, Jr., '36 of the U.S. Army, Lewis B. Cardozo '44 of the Marine Corps and Joseph Thrift '44 of the U.S. Army. Faculty, staff and alumni had served, as the Marine Corps anthem aptly puts it, "in every place and clime where we could take a gun." Vincent and Darbie died in Normandy and France respectively and rest in American military cemeteries with their fellow soldiers. Cardozo was killed in a kamikaze attack aboard USS *Santa Fe* (CL-60) and is memorialized in the Punchbowl Crater National Cemetery in Hawaii. Richie Henderson is entombed in USS *Wahoo* (SS-238), which was lost to depth charging and surface attack in La Perouse Strait, that stormy and treacherous body of water separating Japanese Hokkaido from Russian Sakhalin. Though that sturdy ship and gallant crew was lost in October 1943, the sea did not yield his and his brave shipmates' resting place until 2006. They rest from their labors, entombed and undisturbed, in the wreck of the illustrious ship in which they died, as they have since October 11, 1943.[15] In all but the most unusual circumstances, entombed remains are left undisturbed. The best example of this is the remains of the crew of USS *Arizona* (BB-39) at Pearl Harbor. Sites of this kind are viewed as cemeteries and, except in unique cases such as the USS *Monitor*, are never disturbed. When the turret of the *Monitor* was raised, two sets of skeletal remains were found and sent to the Joint Prisoners of War Missing in Action Command in Hawaii for study and possible identification.

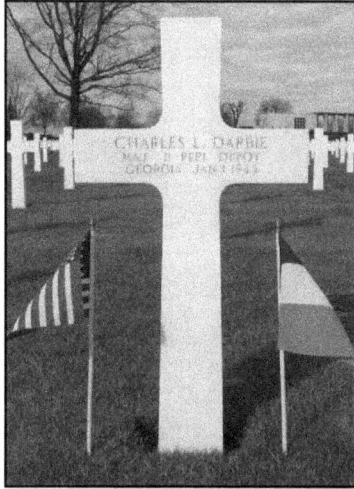

Gravesite of Major Charles L. Darbie '26, USA,
at the American Cemetery, Henri-Chappelle, Belgium
(Courtesy of the American Battle Monuments Commission)

What is important is that members of the Christchurch family served in many places. In some instances, the duty was pedestrian, involving little risk of injury or death. In others, such as Richie Henderson's service aboard the *Wahoo*, the chance of death was enormous. One can only imagine the thoughts that raced through radio operator/gunner Bob Mumper's mind as he prepared to abandon his crippled B-17, which had lost two engines and was shaking itself to destruction as it dove toward the German countryside. One might imagine as well the emotions of Jack Monroe '30 of the 194th Glider Infantry of the 17th Airborne Division as he crossed the Rhine River in a glider as part of Operation Varsity in early 1945. One can consider the service of Thomas L. Grove, M.D., later school physician, an Army doctor assigned to the 28th U.S. Army General Hospital in Egypt. Perhaps one might think of Bob Yarbrough, the legendary ninth headmaster, who served in China in the Army Air Force and later told of watching transport aircraft land in China following long, oftentimes difficult flights across the Himalayas. They set a record of service, when the school was young, and in so doing, provided a stirring example for those who followed. For a time they devoted their lives to defense of the country and served admirably—evidenced by numerous personal and unit awards, attesting to acts of valor and merit, often performed under adverse conditions, in the face of certain death.

It is fitting as we enter the new century to reflect on their deeds, not merely to remember them, but to show how they have established a tradition of service that has been emulated. Selfless, valorous acts such as those of Sergeant Majors, who stayed aboard the crippled aircraft "In Like Errol" to help Bob Mumper put on another parachute, left an indelible mark.[16] In doing this, he enabled the terrified radio operator to escape a gyrating, barely airworthy craft that had lost considerable altitude in a nearly uncontrollable dive. Bob Mumper's faith to "hold on," to sense that he would be spared by a just and loving God, may have been a result of quiet hours in chapel or perhaps the recollection of what Sergeant Joe Farrar '65, who was wounded in Vietnam many years later, termed young boys' raised voices singing praise to Almighty God.[17] Truly those named above, such as Bob Yarbrough, Tom Grove and Bob Mumper, were part of what has become known in our time as the Greatest Generation, and they cannot, must not, be forgotten. As this volume unfolds, we will tell of their service through records of the places and times in which they served, for many of those men are gone now. We will view later service through the oral histories of those who have followed—in Korea, Vietnam, the Caribbean and the Middle East, and in the Continental United States—and in so doing, grasp the common threads of the heritage of service to school and country.

The Chapel in Winter, Christchurch School, 1959 (Author's photographic collection)

From Uncertain Beginnings to Full Victory:
1942–1945

Among those gathered around the radio to hear Franklin Roosevelt request a declaration of war against the Axis powers was Bob Mumper '42, of Hagerstown, Maryland. He enlisted in the Army Air Force not long after finishing the course at Christchurch in June 1942. Still the burden of combat in those early, uncertain days of World War II fell chiefly on older alumni such as Woodford Harwood '23 and John Cook Wyllie '24, who served as a civilian ambulance driver before the United States was officially involved in the war. Wyllie was, according to the evaluation of his superiors, motivated by service to others, perhaps following the example of his father, an Episcopal priest in Chestertown, Maryland.[18] Others, like Tom Marchant '33 and Harry Witzke '34 enlisted in the U.S. Army in the ominous times before Pearl Harbor, while Harry E. Karr, Jr., '36 was called to active duty in the 110th Field Artillery Regiment of the Maryland Army National Guard in February 1941. Elements of the 110th were taken under fire by German shore batteries and could not land until the June 7, 1944, D-Day landings in Normandy. Karr's classmate Sydney A. Vincent, Jr., entered active U.S. Army service in March 1942.

The ground echelon of the 306th Heavy Bombardment Group, also known as "the Reich Wreckers," which included 1st Lieutenant Thomas S. Marchant '33, USAAF, came to the United Kingdom aboard RMS *Queen Elizabeth* in September 1942 to launch the first air attacks on enemy installations in continental Europe in the darkest times of the war. Randy Chowning '42, also in the USAAF, served in the 324th Heavy Bombardment Squadron of the 91st Heavy Bombardment Group, colloquially known as "Wray's Ragged Irregulars," which arrived in England later and began combat missions in November 1942. Randy "Dolph" Chowning '42 did not arrive until June 15, 1944, and flew as a flight engineer/top turret gunner in B-17 serial number 42-97959, nicknamed "Rhapsody in Red." Men of Christchurch, such as Jack Monroe '30, crossed the Rhine in glider aircraft, while others waited for the day of victory and liberation from German prisoner of war camps. Because many are no longer with us, we know of their deeds and achievements, not from their own statements and recollections but rather from the records of the commands in which they served and the testimonies of those who served with them. Much is written in citations for personal awards attesting to great heroism and substantial meritorious conduct. One can learn a great deal of the milieu in which these fine young men served by reading what was written contemporaneously in recommendations for personal awards for bravery and meritorious service.[19]

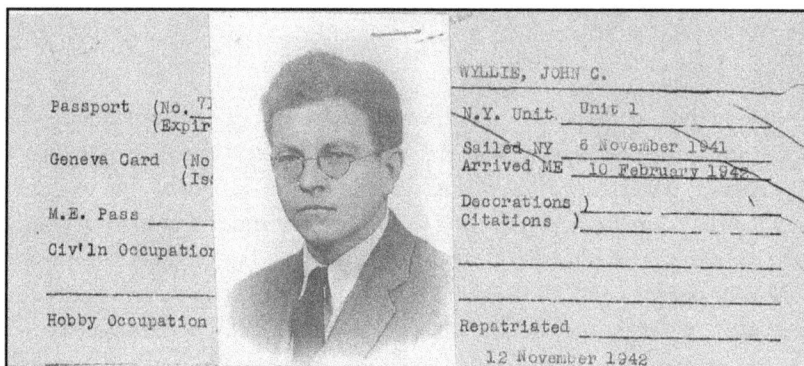

Lieutenant John Cook Wyllie '24, USAAF, shown as an ambulance driver of the American Field Service (1941–42) (Courtesy Archives of the American Field Service and AFS Intercultural Programs)

Aircrew of B-17 aircraft nicknamed "Rhapsody in Red." T/Sergeant V. Randolph Chowning second row, middle (Official U.S. Army photograph)

The squadrons of the 306th Heavy Bombardment Group, which served as inspiration for the novel and movie *Twelve O'Clock High,* were the first to fly bombing missions over occupied Europe. Early raids did not reach into the German homeland, and it was not until later in the war that long-range, full-scale daylight bombing began.

On the morning of December 20, 1942, 1st Lieutenant J. R. McKee, USAAF, with 1st Lieutenant Thomas S. Marchant '33, USAAF, as his navigator, turned up the engines in USAAF A/C number 41-24495 to begin mission number 26, the 367th Heavy Bombardment Squadron's daylight bombing of a German Luftwaffe Air Depot at Romilly sur Seine near Paris in occupied France. The mission was to inflict as much damage as possible on the Nazi air depot located in this town. The raid did not involve deep penetration of enemy-occupied territory. It did involve eighty B-17 aircraft, six of which were lost in action. One airman was reported killed in action (KIA), four were wounded (WIA) and twenty-nine, including Lieutenants McKee and Marchant, were carried as missing in action (MIA).

Missing crew list from B-17 aircraft number 41-24495 for raid over Romilly-sur-Seine, France, December 20, 1942. (Courtesy 306th Heavy Bombardment Group Association)

Early during the course of the mission, Tom Marchant was wounded by enemy gunfire. Subsequently, while bailing out of the aircraft,[20] he fractured his arm and was treated by German doctors, who removed bone from his lower leg and used wires to repair the arm fracture. After the war, he told his son that while hospitalized he was offered a rat for a meal and declined it; he said that later on he was so hungry, he might well have eaten it![21] Those on board the McKee aircraft were declared missing, for the crew in a nearby aircraft did not actually see the aircraft go down.[22] They spent the remainder of the war in Stalag Luft Three, at Sagan, southeast of Berlin, a POW camp for allied airmen made famous in the movie *The Great Escape*.[23] When seeing the film, Tom spoke to his eldest son of his incarceration, quietly saying, "I was there; we all built tunnels."[24] As the Russian Army advanced on Berlin, the prisoners were force-marched toward Nuremberg, and ultimately Tom Marchant was returned to Allied custody on May 30, 1945. He married after the war and eventually settled in Middlesex County, Virginia, not far from where he was born. He died in 1995 and rests alongside Bill Jones '28, Everett Blake '32, Mick Bowman '42 and Taliaferro Bargamin '56 as well as Christian Willaford, who was proprietor of the school store and barber for many years and served in the U.S. Navy. There are four other alumni veterans, one former faculty member and two employees buried in Christ Church Cemetery among stately trees and often gently worn markers, down the road from the school. Tom declined compensation for his injuries and retired from a successful career in the insurance business.

Captain Thomas S. Marchant '33, USAAF, in 1946 (Courtesy of Thomas S. Marchant, Jr.)

The early slow pace of Allied air operations over occupied Europe quickened. As part of the increased operational tempo, Sergeant "Dolph" Chowning '42 and his aircraft, "Rhapsody in Red" of the 324th Heavy Bombardment Squadron, arrived in June 1944 and rapidly got into action. A week after arrival, on June 22, 1944, Lieutenant Collins and his crew departed on a mission to destroy an electrical transformer station at Mazingarbe, France, which was unsuccessful because the novice aircraft commander could not locate the formation headed for the target. However, by August 4, 1944, the aircrew had overcome its initial false start and, with Lieutenant Lawrence Gaddis at the controls, participated on a difficult mission to destroy a hydrogen peroxide fuel processing plant at Peenemunde, Usedom Island, Germany, on the Baltic Sea, the site of highly sensitive, secret development of the V-1 "buzz bombs" that had rained down on London, Antwerp, Lille and Maastricht in 1944.

Completing missions against the facility was made more urgent by the concurrent development of V-2 rockets, which could be moved from one launch site to another without great difficulty and were harder to counter. The squadron operation report notes that a second raid was needed to complete destruction of an earlier attack. Severely damaged by anti-aircraft fire in this raid, Rhapsody did not return to action until late August 1944, when she and other bombers attacked German airfields at Kolleda and Goslar. In all, Rhapsody completed ninety-five missions over Northern Europe. Her most harrowing mission—the last of the 91st Bomb Group on April 25, 1945—was to strike a Nazi airfield and the Skoda Armaments Factory southwest of Pilsen, Czechoslovakia. In that final mission, the war-weary plane was so badly struck by flak that her electrical and hydraulic systems were disabled, and her landing gear had to be lowered by hand. She returned to England alone on reduced power because one engine was out and another not pulling full power. The mission commander refused her pilot permission to land at Alconbury, where there were longer runways. She reached home station at Bassingbourn and barely landed safely. The aircraft and her crew returned to the United States in late May 1945, and Sergeant Chowning later mused that after repeatedly risking his life in combat over northern Europe, he found it impossible upon his return to the United States to order a beer, for he was underage.

Lieutenant Richie Henderson '35, deemed by his Annapolis classmates to be a "born sailor possessing ingenuity and good common sense,"[25] served aboard one of the most illustrious submarines in the United States Navy, USS *Wahoo* (SS-238), which in her short career sank twenty Japanese ships in six war patrols. The key ingredient in this record was Commander Dudley W. "Mush" Morton, USN, a fearless leader who was not afraid to take the ship into Japanese home waters and to operate aggressively in contrast to earlier submarine skippers

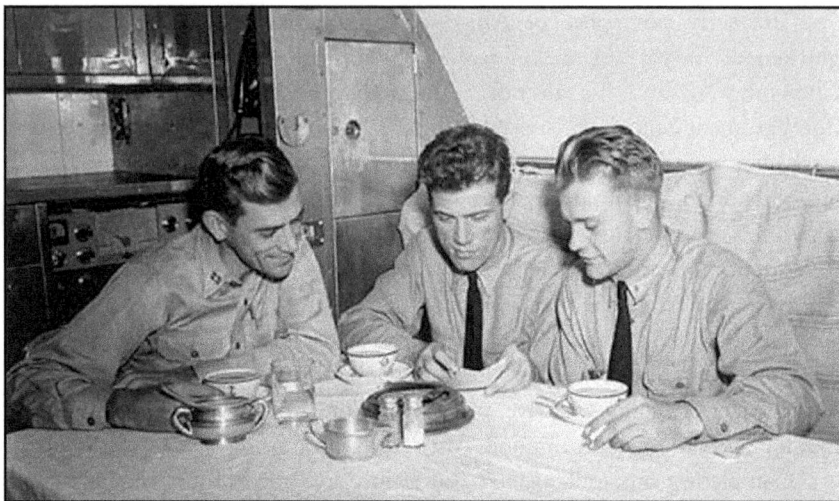

Lieutenant Richie N. Henderson '35, USN, Lieutenant Chandler Jackson, USN, and Ensign John Campbell, USN, in the wardroom of USS Wahoo *(SS-238) (Courtesy USS* Bowfin *(SS-287) Museum*

who had been comparatively timid. In fact, Morton's immediate predecessor, Lieutenant Commander Marvin Granville Kennedy, USN, had been thought less aggressive, and on the ship's first war patrol, two large targets, a mother ship for midget submarines and an aircraft carrier, had been passed by. In his written evaluation of the patrol report, known in the Navy as an endorsement, the commander of Submarine Squadron Ten had criticized Kennedy for failure to attack these enemy ships. A fertile hunting ground was the Sea of Japan and its approaches, which were entered by transiting La Perouse Strait, a cold, often stormy and treacherous body of water between Japanese Hokkaido and Russian Sakhalin. The strait was protected by shore batteries, a minefield and nearby airfields at Wakkani[26] and Otaro, from which air attacks might be launched. In September 1943, *Wahoo* began her patrol in company with USS *Sawfish* (SS-276).[27]

Little is known of what happened on the ill-fated patrol. There is some indication that *Wahoo* sank four Japanese ships, but she began her outward voyage eleven days before the scheduled end of patrol. It has been speculated that she had used all her torpedoes or had perhaps been so severely damaged that she had to return home. No one really knows what happened to cause the ship to leave the area.

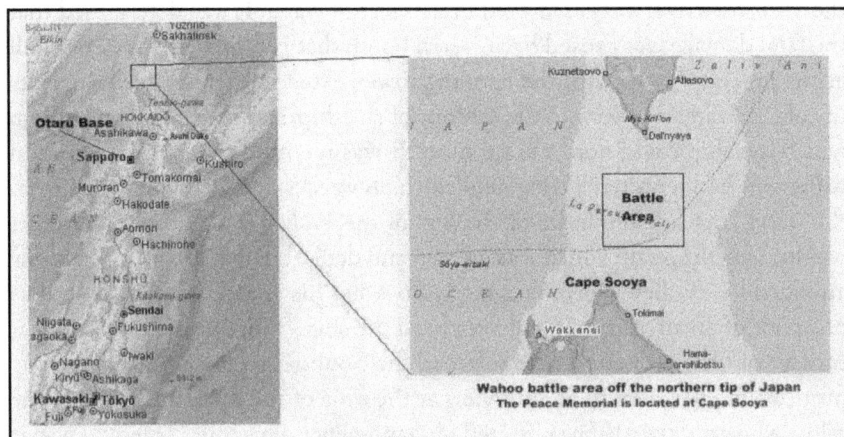

Map/diagram of La Perouse Strait (Courtesy USS Bowfin (SS-287) Museum)

What is known is that Captain Morton attempted a daylight passage through the strait, was taken under fire, damaged by shore batteries and submerged. In the early morning and throughout the day of October 11, 1943, she was repeatedly attacked by shore-based Japanese aircraft and changed course to the northwest as if to make for the Soviet Union, not then at war with Japan, where the crew would be interned. Later reports and contemporaneous photographs document her destruction, after about twenty sorties. The attack narrative and photos were discovered many years later by Vice Admiral Kazuo Ueda, a retired officer of the Japanese Maritime Self Defense Force, and show the oil trailing from the mortally damaged ship. The photographs are haunting, and it is difficult to imagine the thoughts of those in the crippled submarine, who must have sensed after repeated aerial bombardment that the end might well be near.

Drawing of fatal damage to USS Wahoo (SS-238)
(Courtesy USS Bowfin (SS-287) Museum)

Many years later, in 2006, as part of oil/mineral exploration near Sakhalin, the *Wahoo's* wreck was discovered in 213 feet of water. It was determined that the fatal damage was caused by an aerial bomb that ruptured the pressure hull at the junction point with the conning tower, extending to the keel. Torrents of cold seawater rushed into the interior of the ship, a catastrophic injury from which the ship could not have survived. It was reported that since 1943 local fisherman had reported having nets "catch" in wrecks at that point. Apart from the wreck, the sole reminder of the loss of the *Wahoo* is a granite monument overlooking the strait, which was erected and dedicated in 1995, in a ceremony attended by Dudley Morton's aging widow and his granddaughter, as well as one pilot of an aircraft that had destroyed the ship. Those present related that passage of time seemed to have softened the wounds and losses of that fall day fifty-two years earlier. In an interview at the time of the dedication, one of the pilots who attacked *Wahoo* reflected for a moment on his role: "During a war, it is kill or be killed . . . whomever (sic) finds the enemy first wins . . . We had no personal hate toward any of them . . ."

Other members of the Christchurch family served in desperate combat operations in the initial phases of recapture of Europe. These operations played out in the November 1942 invasion of North Africa and follow on evolutions in the mountains of Tunisia, where initial Allied losses at Kasserine Pass imperiled success of attaining the overriding goal—ejecting Italian and German forces from the African continent. Operations at sea involved unrestricted submarine warfare against maritime forces of the Empire of Japan, on which Lieutenant Richie Henderson, USN, was lost in the destruction of USS *Wahoo* (SS-238) in the early fall of 1943. Captain Sydney Vincent, Jr., '36, USA, of the 803rd Tank Destroyer Battalion, gave his life in July 1944 in the fierce fighting at the Battle of St. Lo in Normandy. He volunteered to destroy a German observation post near his unit's command post and was killed by mortar and sniper fire.

Grave site of Captain Sydney A. Vincent, Jr., '36 USA, at the American Cemetery, Colleville-sur-Mer, Normandy, France (Courtesy of American Battle Monuments Commission)

While Allied leaders who met at the Arcadia Conference[28] of Christmas tide 1941–1942 decided that offensive operations in Europe were to have priority in the prosecution of global conflict, hostilities in the Pacific were not neglected. Robertson Langley-Wood '42, known to his classmates as "Doc," entered the Navy in May 1943 and served as a radioman striker on USS *Belknap* (APD-34), a World War I vintage "four pipe" destroyer that served successively as a converted seaplane tender and high-speed amphibious transport. He recalled convoy-type duty escorting fleet oiler USS *Aucilla* (AO-56)[29] to Baytown, Texas, for a fuel lift to Trinidad, and returning to the United States with ammunition ship USS *Nitro* (AE-2).

After transiting the Panama Canal, the ship transported Underwater Demolition Team (UDT) members to invasion sites where they performed beach surveys and cleared any obstructions they found. Just two days after Christmas 1944, *Belknap* got underway from Hollandia, West New Guinea, to support operations involving the landings at Lingayen on Luzon Island in the Philippines. Underwater Demolition Team Nine was aboard on January 6, 1945, as the Battle of the Bulge was winding down in Europe, with the ship providing covering shore bombardment for pre-landing UDT evolutions near the town of Lingayen. On that day, ships gunners had destroyed two attacking enemy aircraft. On January 10, 1945, suicide watercraft and Japanese swimmers tried to attack the ship with hand grenades, and eleven were promptly dispatched by small arms fire from *Belknap* crew members, but the worst was yet to come.

On the 12th, while off the transport area of the "green beach" landing area, the ship was struck by a kamikaze aircraft, which demolished the number-two smokestack and two assault boats and killed thirty-nine sailors. Langley-Wood was among the forty-nine wounded.[30] The old ship was so severely damaged that she lost power, lay at anchor until January 18, 1945, and had to be towed over open ocean by fleet tug USS *Hidatsa* (ATF-102) to Manus Island for temporary repair. She was repaired so that she could return to San Diego, California, and after a close inspection, it was decided that she should sail to Philadelphia for decommissioning and disposal.[31] At the same time, "Doc" began the long process of recovering from his wounds in shore-side naval hospitals and was ultimately discharged at Fort Eustis, Virginia, in October 1945.

By July 1944, Allied forces in Italy had entered Rome, and those in Northern Europe had gained a firm foothold in rural Normandy in France. However, strong Nazi resistance had temporarily stymied the progress of the invasion forces in the deceptively bucolic countryside. A key ingredient in breaking the stalemate was capture of the city of Saint Lo, a major transportation and road junction. This was done concurrently with the initiation of Operation Cobra, a decisive step led by Generals Omar Bradley and George S. Patton, conceived to permit a drive to the Seine River and thence into Germany. Fierce fighting continued for nearly a month, and that city was nearly destroyed by aerial bombardment and street-to-street and house-to-house combat. Troops of the 29th Division, supported by the 803rd Tank Destroyer Battalion to which Captain Sydney A. Vincent, Jr., '36, USA, was assigned, pounded the Germans defending St. Lo into submission. These were the same troops who had earned a lasting niche in history with the sacrifice of the Bedford Boys at the water's edge on June 6, 1944.[32]

On July 19, 1944, as Captain Vincent and his men entered that embattled city, he was mortally wounded by Nazi mortar and sniper fire as he and his M10 Tank Destroyer crew tried to destroy a German observation post. Decorated for heroism with the Silver Star and Purple Heart, he rests with his comrades in the American Cemetery overlooking the English Channel at Colleville-sur-Mer.[33]

Christmas season in 1944 was an unexpectedly perilous time for Allied forces in Europe and, as events unfolded, became one of dark foreboding and uncertainty, not merely for those in combat in Europe and elsewhere, but also for those in the United States who were having their fourth wartime holiday. On December 3, Thalhimer's department store advertised in the *Richmond Times-Dispatch*, the Virginia city's morning newspaper, gifts for a "Sentimental Christmas," among them a "Hickock leather belt for $3.50." It seemed that the nation had been lulled into a false sense of security by Allied successes and German political deterioration, war weariness and smoldering discontent. That favorable view of the war's progress was abruptly shattered in mid December.

Though the invasion forces—which included Christchurch alumni Harry Witzke, Frank B. Tavenner, Jim Davenport and Sydney Vincent— had encountered the temporary setbacks described earlier, the momentum of operations had been regained. Nazi invaders had been driven from most of Italy, and Allied forces had driven through the Rhone Valley following the landings in Southern France at St. Tropez and San Rafael, in a maneuver known as Operation Dragoon. Moreover, a cabal of disaffected German officers, which included Admiral Wilhelm Canaris, head of the Abwehr intelligence organization, and Field Marshal Erwin Rommel, the famed Desert Fox, had on July 20, 1944, carried out a plot to assassinate Adolf Hitler at his field headquarters known as Wolfschanze in a forest in East Prussia. They felt that if Hitler were killed, they might sue for a separate peace with the Western Allies.

That abortive plot, known by the code word Valkyrie, failed because it was carried out in a frame building rather than the usual underground bunker conference room, and because the briefcase containing the bomb was placed behind a stout table leg by another staff officer who was not among the plotters and did not know its contents, thus blocking the force of the explosion.

Supplies to support the drive across formerly occupied Europe came in increasing amounts through the recently liberated port of Antwerp, Belgium. All conventional indications by mid-December 1944 were that Hitler and his cronies were facing certain defeat in the near future. German military leadership, from the top down, was completely demoralized in the aftermath of the assassination attempt. Military personnel were required to use the party greeting—"Heil Hitler"—rather than traditional military salutes. Hitler and die-hard Nazis initiated a strong cleansing program to root out and destroy those tainted by participation in the abortive plot.

The most talented officers in the Army were lost. For example, Field Marshal Rommel, the famed Desert Fox, committed suicide rather than face the "justice" meted out by the so-called "Peoples Court" to the broken men brought before its foul-mouthed leader, Richard Freisler. Admiral Canaris was imprisoned at Floessenburg until early April 1945, when he was dragged naked from his cell and hanged, along with Dietrich Bonhoeffer, the German theologian who was implicated in an earlier plot to kill Hitler. Nearly five hundred souls were arrested[34], and two hundred executed in the scourge, thus breaking organized resistance to Hitler. In some case, films of those executed— in their death throes—were made for the despot to watch. Wehrmacht generals were subjected to extraordinary scrutiny and their personal sidearms were taken from them before staff conferences at which Hitler and other political figures were present.

Though the way ahead seemed favorable to the West by late 1944, Allied commanders such as General Eisenhower and Field Marshal Montgomery did not know that Hitler and his military acolytes had developed a plan that was to be carried out in mid-December 1944. The German High Command named it Operation Watch on the Rhine, after a patriotic German hymn; but it was to be known as the Battle of the Bulge among the Western Allies. The objective was to drive between the First and Third Armies and capture Antwerp, depriving Allied troops of needed logistic support. Again, those in charge in Germany felt they could come to surrender terms with those in power in the West, rather than having to deal with the Russians as well. The German force was overwhelming, and the Nazis used deceptive tactics, such as traveling in captured American vehicles, changing road signs, severing communication lines and using native-English-speaking German troops.

The attack, which began on December 16, 1944, was made under the cover of fog, snow and inclement weather. Virginia's *Richmond Times-Dispatch* December 18, 1944, issue noted in bold headlines: "German Drive Engulfs First Army, Smashes into Belgium and Luxembourg." The situation was uncertain and a "news blackout" raised fears that the German drive might jeopardize

Allied progress. Jim Davenport '42 and his classmates Frank Tavenner and Bill Bowman were in front-line commands that bore the brunt of the German offensive.

Bowman, who was severely wounded on February 10, 1945, was a member of the 345th Infantry Regiment of the 87th Infantry Division. The regiment had entered the Saar in Germany when the unexpected offensive began. American troops, stunned by the ferocity of the attack, initially fell back. In one of the greatest atrocities of the war, SS troops of Kampfgruppe Peiper, on December 17, 1944, summarily executed eighty-four American soldiers near Malmedy, Belgium, and left their corpses in the snow. They were later found by Allied forces that recaptured the lost territory.

These unexpected stealth attacks, often carried out by Germans in American uniforms who spoke unaccented idiomatic English, were devastating, and Allied troops retreated. In a move that proved critical, the retreating forces destroyed fuel dumps, effectively devastating the Germans' hope of taking Antwerp. On December 18th, an unsigned editorial in the *Richmond Times-Dispatch* opined,

> The force of this offensive makes it plain that the Germans are far from broken . . . The strength and determination that the German Army is showing should convince us all that the end is not in sight.

Moreover, the weather on the European continent was reported to be dreadful, the coldest winter in many years. Our troops were lashed by intermittent rain and snow and were often poorly clothed and unprepared for the rigors of winter. Fog and poor visibility initially prevented air interdiction operations. In fact, an aircraft in which Sergeant Randy "Dolph" Chowning '42 was a top turret gunner crashed near Shepreth, England, on its Christmas Eve 1944 takeoff from RAF Bassingbourn, an air station near Cambridge, on a mission against a German airfield at Kirchgoens, Germany. Years later, he recalled the smell of gasoline fumes from ruptured fuel lines and "spraying down the engines" to prevent the sparks from igniting a major fire.

As if in response to the prayerful intercession of General Patton's Third Army chaplain, Colonel James H. O'Neill, the turning point in the Battle of the Bulge came on December 23, 1944, when the fog lifted and "immoderate" snow and rains stopped, thus permitting offensive air operations against the German horde.[35]

Tom Brokaw, the noted television journalist and author, recounted his emotions from a June 1984 trip to Normandy as he prepared a television documentary on the fortieth anniversary observance of the June 6, 1944, D-Day landings. He recalled walking along the beach with sixty- and seventy-year-old men whose stories he heard, who had returned in some cases with their families to see, some of them perhaps for the last time, the site of their great triumph over adversity. This was where many of their comrades had died, at the water's edge or on the beaches. As President Reagan put it in a memorable speech on the cliff at Pointe du Hoc overlooking the English Channel, "They came to seize back the continent of Europe." Brokaw was, he said, "profoundly grateful for all they had done," and set out to memorialize that thankfulness. He described the characteristics and traits of the men and women in a book he called *The Greatest Generation.* They were

> United not only by a common purpose but by common values . . . duty, honor . . . service to country and above all . . . by responsibility to oneself . . . (Their) everyday lives reveal how they persevered through the war and were trained by it . . .

Perhaps more significantly, Brokaw noted that they were self-effacing about their individual achievements. They believed they were, he said, "doing what everyone else was doing." Brokaw observed, "It was almost impossible to get them to talk about their combat experiences."[36] Because they were occupied with securing educations and resuming civilian careers, it was not until many years later that they had the chance to reflect on the meaning of lives of so long ago. For example, Ray Winder '42, in recalling his service in the Army Air Force as a pilot trainee and later a waist gunner in a B-17, said it "was surely unremarkable and undistinguished." He compared his service to that of his friends and classmates such as "Dolph" Chowning, who survived a B-17 crash, and "Doc" Langley-Wood, who narrowly escaped death at Lingayen.

Though those in the school family served in different venues and with different assignments and different degrees of danger, all contributed to the ultimate victory. Later faculty member Fred Riley commanded a Coastal Patrol converted yacht USS *Sapphire* (PYc-2), whose crew rescued survivors of the torpedoed merchant ship SS *Plow City* in lifeboats two hundred miles east of Atlantic City, New Jersey, and later served on USS *Gunnel* (SS-253), a submarine commanded by Senator John McCain's father that carried the war to the Japanese home waters. In the third war patrol, the ship observed the so-called Tokyo-Truk route from a point somewhat to the southwest of the Tokyo Bay entrance, and in the evenings listened to propaganda broadcasts of Tokyo Rose, who told them on December 17, 1943, in her dulcet voice, that they knew where *Gunnel* was and that she would be "sent to Davy Jones locker." In fact, contrary to Ray Winder's observation, no service was insignificant, a fact that Brokaw has explicitly and repeatedly recognized in recent years.

It is perfectly clear that these members of the Christchurch family were members of "the greatest generation" too, persevered in the war, and went on to productive lives after the war. One person who exemplified this trait was James S. G. Davenport '42, who went on to contribute to his community as chairman of the Newport News, Virginia, Planning Commission, in working for the Boy Scouts of America and for the United Way of his community.[37] In their time in the service, he and others very likely gained a clear realization of their own mortality at an early age, often by seeing death and destruction around them. They were required to endure privation and danger that might end in death— as it had for Richie Henderson, quickly, in a terrible explosion that ruptured the pressure hull of his ship and admitted torrents of onrushing cold water. It was a realization that brought maturity, and it came in the skies over Europe and aboard ships in the Atlantic and the Southwest Pacific—very different venues from the quiet chapel with sometimes-creaking floorboards and pews, and from the green lawn in front of the headmaster's home overlooking the wide, gently flowing river. It may be that memories of a more tranquil time in the sanctuary of the chapel or on the bank of the river sustained those who served, and gave those who were lost a sense of peace at the end.

A New Kind of Conflict
The Long Cold War

As noted earlier in discussing the plight of Allied aviators held in Stalag Luft One, the coalition fashioned by the Allied powers seemed to disintegrate as World War II drew to a close. The dissolution of the wartime alliance began at the Yalta Conference, code-named Argonaut, held in the Crimea between the 4th and 11th of February 1945. President Franklin Roosevelt, who was gravely ill and exhausted, was able to maintain the alliance only with major territorial concessions made at Yalta. Additionally, it was stipulated that the Soviet-sponsored "Lublin Government" was to control Poland, subject to later free elections. Further, the Soviet government was able to secure other concessions, including not initiating hostilities with Japan until the war was very nearly over. Prime Minister Stalin was no longer viewed as a benevolent figure, and Russian hegemony over Eastern European nations was very quickly established and maintained until 1989.

In his eloquent landmark speech at Westminster College in Fulton, Missouri, Winston Churchill, Britain's wartime prime minister, spoke of the "Iron Curtain" that had abruptly fallen across Eastern Europe, a precursor of what became known as the Cold War. This conflict was to be a lengthy, insidious struggle, characterized by attempts at subversion of legitimate governments and frequently punctuated by open violent conflict. In some cases, however, the armed forces engaged in activities of a more subtle nature.

Former Christchurch academic dean Robert C. Goodman, Jr., was a member of the 7721st Broadcast and Leaflet company of the U.S. Army at Heidelberg, Germany. One function of the command was to prepare for contingency operations involving Russian military invasion of Poland. This entailed research of modern European history, which revealed that Russian forces had invaded Poland twenty-three times in the course of recorded history. The unit's members, Goodman recalled, prepared leaflets stating that "the Russians are not your friends," or words to that effect, to be dropped over Poland in case the invasion materialized. They were involved in other planning activities, in anticipation of major regional armed conflict. He recalled with amusement that he and others in the headquarters were involved in the logistics planning of the evacuation of military dependents that would be required if Russian forces invaded Germany. The planners concluded that such an operation would be virtually impossible because mass evacuation would cause catastrophic traffic jams on German highways.[38]

The struggle was initially played out among nations whose populations had just endured a protracted war. Armies and fleets had been disbanded, and those released from armed struggle wanted consumer goods, and to return to homes and schooling; they wished for disengagement rather than a continuation of the recently ended war. There was little realization that this was a serious conflict. Whittaker Chambers, senior editor of *Time* magazine, put it this way:

> It is part of the failure of the West to understand that it is at grips with an enemy having no moral viewpoint in common with itself, that two irreconcilable viewpoints . . . of man's fate and the future are involved and hence their conflict is irrepressible . . . [39]

In summary, during the Cold War, there was an ongoing threat of military action. It was combined with the incomprehensible, perverse attraction of Communist ideology that proved the undoing of otherwise highly intelligent people such as Alger Hiss. He was the patrician government official convicted for perjury in testifying to Congress about passing sensitive documents to the Russians.[40]

President Harry Truman—who was initially seen by some, accustomed to the polish of his predecessor, as a somewhat bumbling, unworthy successor to Franklin Roosevelt—was by no means the ingénue he was assumed to be. On April 25th, 1945, before the war in Europe was over (let alone the war in the Pacific), Truman upbraided Soviet Foreign Minister Molotov when it became obvious that the Russians would not honor certain portions of the Yalta agreements, such as the one involving Poland.[41] In so doing, he showed a stubborn determination to oppose communism over the course of many years, should that be required.

In general, the period was one of chronic political instability and economic warfare, with wars waged by surrogates of the United States and the Soviet Union. The new war played out in a variety of locations: Greece, Berlin, Korea, Hungary, Cuba and Vietnam, to name a few. It brought with it new forms of combat. President Truman, who proved his mettle and his alertness to the threat, initially poured considerable money into Greece to prevent the fall of a free government. Meanwhile, General George C. Marshall, USA, America's preeminent soldier-statesman in 1947, fashioned the European Recovery Plan (ERP) (which would ultimately bear his name) to rebuild Western Europe to include Germany.

There was ample back-and-forth during these tumultuous times. It could be argued that the 1948–49 blockade of West Berlin, in which surface traffic to that isolated city was severely restricted, was a response to Marshall's efforts. The United States and other Allied powers mounted a massive effort known as Operation Vittles, which provided the wherewithal to feed and fuel the city, and ultimately broke the Russian blockade. In 1950, North Koreans, who were subsequently aided by Chinese communists, invaded South Korea, eliciting an American response known by some as a "police action," which resulted in a stalemate. The fact that hostilities still technically exist influences our present-day actions, such as the residual United States military presence in South Korea. French Colonial rulers were ejected from North Vietnam after the battle and extended siege at Dien Bien Phu in 1954, and the United States Navy created a task force named the Passage to Freedom to evacuate indigenous Vietnamese from the area north of the 17th parallel to safety, which was ultimately stymied when communists took over that entire embattled land. The operating theory was the Truman Doctrine of "containment," the notion that subversion must be confined or contained to specific geographic areas.

Beginning in 1956, guerilla forces in Cuba, under the direction of their leader, Fidel Castro, and initially based in the Sierra Maestra Mountains of Oriente Province close to the U.S. Naval base at Guantanamo Bay, conducted continuous insurgency operations, forcing the departure of the despot Fulgencio Batista. The promise of the revolution was compromised by Castro and his henchmen, an eventuality not anticipated by those like Eduardo Gonzales '59 and George Montalvan '60, whose grandfather, the Reverend Mr. F. Ernest Warren, founded Christchurch.

The world came close to thermonuclear war in the fall of 1962, when it was discovered that Russians, acting in conjunction with their vassal state and its rogue leader, had begun to install Intercontinental Ballistic Missiles (ICBMs) on Cuba. In late October, President Kennedy imposed a strict quarantine on maritime shipments bound for Cuba,[42] enforced by ships of the United States Navy.

On the evening of the October 22, 1962, as the president spoke to a stunned, anxious nation on live television, USS *Newport News* (CA-148) and USS *Leary* (DD-879) hurriedly left their homeport at Norfolk, Virginia. They were later joined by other destroyers from East Coast ports, including USS *Joseph P. Kennedy Jr.* (DD-850) named for the president's late brother. The *Kennedy*, along with USS *John R. Pierce* (DD-753), sent boarding parties to SS *Marucla*, a Lebanese merchantman under charter to the Soviet Government. The parties inspected her and found no prohibited cargo. The ships formed two lines, nicknamed *Walnut* and *Chestnut*, to track, and, if need be, to turn back Soviet bloc ships carrying offensive weapons. These surface ships were supplemented by reconnaissance aircraft. The American armed forces were placed on the alert status known as DEFCON 3, which was later raised to DEFCON 2. After thirteen days, the Soviet leader chose to remove the missiles. It was a perilous time. Subsequently, the president ordered the removal of obsolete Jupiter Missiles from Turkey, though the withdrawal was not to be regarded as quid pro quo.

USS Corry (DDR-817) *refueling alongside USS* Baltimore (CA-68) (*Courtesy USS* Corry (DD-817) *Association*

Darkness falls quickly after spectacularly lovely sunsets in the tropics, and the early evening of July 15, 1963, was no exception. At dusk on that moonless, warm night, the crew of the USS *Corry* (DDR-817), which had earlier been involved in the initial response to the Cuban Missile Crisis in October 1962,[43] set sea detail and got underway from the naval station at Key West, Florida, on a tracking mission to locate a Russian merchantman thought to have contraband cargo on board. The ship, one of the last in the quarantine line, steamed to a point more than three miles off the Cuban coast between Mariel Bay and Havana harbor. Komar torpedo boats came out near the *Corry* but did not otherwise molest or challenge her.

At a point well into the mid-watch, radar operators in the ship's combat information center (CIC) were startled by a shrill wail in their ECM (electronic countermeasures) gear, denoting that the ship had been detected and "painted" by fire-control radar based ashore. Using three direction finder bearings, it didn't take long for the watch team to determine that the radar was located on a mobile missile battery most likely emplaced on a railway flatcar on the outskirts of Havana. It was an abrupt reminder that, as Albert Einstein once observed, the world was an untidy and dangerous place, even though the mortal peril of the fall of 1962 seemed past to those on board. The ship's company on that dark, balmy night included Sandy Monroe '60, an NROTC midshipman on board for summer cruise. As one sailor, Radarman 2nd Class James Shaftic, USN, on the *Corry* that night, recalled it,

> At 4 am I was relieved of the watch and hit the rack knowing that if somebody pushed the button in Havana, the *Corry* would be hit by a missile . . . Naval Intelligence wanted our trace and sound tape of the Fire Can radar, and we sent them to D.C. *Corry* got a BZ (Well done) from Intel.[44]

These times, which were often unsettled and turbulent, required maintaining large standing armed forces against unpredictable contingencies for extended periods, a melancholy reality noted by John F. Kennedy in a speech at American University in June 1963.

The first fatality of what became known as the Vietnam War was Richard B. Fitzgibbon of Stoneham, Massachusetts, who was killed on June 8, 1956, a little more than six months after the establishment of the Military Assistance Advisory Group (MAAG) Vietnam on November 1, 1955. In an inexorable fashion, the scope and intensity of the conflict grew, amidst byplay about whether it was a civil war among competing Vietnamese factions or part of a larger and more sinister insurgency—colloquially known by some as the "domino theory." It was thought—not without justification—that if a resolute stand was not taken in Vietnam, Southeast Asia would fall to international Communist domination.

Ensign H. Murrell McLeod '58, USN at Newport, R.I., 1962 (Courtesy H. Murrell McLeod)

The original notion was that by sending advisors and logistic support of one variety and another, the South Vietnamese government could be sustained and enhanced to the point that the partitioned nation might survive. In the early stage of the conflict, American ships such as the aircraft carrier USS *Hancock* (CVA-19), on which Lieutenant (Junior Grade) Murrell McLeod '58, USN, served, carried barrels of the herbicide Agent Orange used in the Operation Ranch Hand defoliation of the Vietnamese countryside, with long-term devastating outcomes. Some of the containers had "rotted out," and Murrell and his sailors had the chore of rolling them overboard and, in the process, became soiled with the dusty preparation.

Gradually, however, the pace of counterinsurgency accelerated. One of the first marines to serve in Vietnam was Colonel (then Captain) James T. Breckinridge '42, USMC, who was assigned as an advisor, or "Co Van," to the nascent Vietnamese Marine Corps. Following the Gulf of Tonkin Resolution in the late summer 1964, the U.S. moved headlong into war.

A conflict that began as a well-intentioned, noble adventure ended some twenty years later after the expenditure of over 58,000 young men and women whose names are memorialized on the Vietnam Memorial. It was a tragic, lengthy interlude,[45] and its results touched families from places as remote and isolated as tiny Tangier Island in the Chesapeake Bay to Arlington National Cemetery, the hallowed and lovely last resting place of Lieutenant Lewis B. Puller, Jr., '63, USMC, who died many years after his Vietnam service.

Captain William Dabney '53, USMC, who retired in 1990 as a colonel, played a vital role in the defense of the combat base at Khe Sanh. Bill Dabney and four hundred of his comrades from India Company, Third Battalion, Twenty Sixth Marines, held Hill 881 South against a regimental-sized North Vietnamese (NVA) opposing force for seventy-seven days. Their position was completely isolated and could be resupplied and reinforced only by helicopters of HMM364 (Marine Medium Helicopter Squadron 364), nicknamed "The Purple Foxes," itself a risky undertaking for the aviators. This was underscored by the fact that in the first thirty days on the hill, seven of the squadron's aircraft were lost to enemy fire. Marines brought in as replacements had to move from the helicopters to the trenches quickly to avoid being targeted by the NVA forces below. Dabney later described somewhat wryly the sole sapper attack and noted, "The only thing it proved was that a Marine could throw a grenade downhill much better than NVA troops could throw them uphill, and they went away . . ."[46]

*Colonel William H. Dabney '53, USMC (Collections
of the Preston Library, Virginia Military Institute)*

Had the hill fallen, NVA troops could have occupied the heights and bombarded the main combat base and airfield at will, repeating the tragedy at Dien Bien Phu, which was a precursor to French abandonment of Vietnam and partition of the country fourteen years earlier. Under Dabney's exemplary leadership, the marines endured and thus became legendary in the Corps. In later years, he recalled that each morning of the seventy-seven-day interlude, volunteers, risking their lives to incoming mortar fire, observed morning colors in full view of their NVA tormentors.

In the end, Hill 881 did not fall, and though the main base at Khe Sanh was abandoned in July 1968, it was no longer tactically required. In an omission that somehow happens in wartime, the paperwork for Bill Dabney's Navy Cross was lost, and the well-earned decoration was bestowed in a formal ceremony at the Virginia Military Institute on April 15, 2005, in the company of other survivors of the three-month ordeal from both India Company and HMM364.

Bill Dabney's brother-in-law, Second Lieutenant Lewis B. Puller, Jr., '63, USMC, was not so fortunate. Some six months after the siege of Khe Sanh, on October 11, 1968, Lewis Puller, Jr., was grievously wounded when he stepped on a booby-trapped howitzer shell, which exploded and carried with it both of his legs and portions of his hands. Though severely wounded, the valiant officer continued to direct his men from the litter to which he was taken prior to being medically evacuated. Lew Puller struggled in a different fashion through long, painful months of hospitalization and rehabilitation. In the words of Bob Yarbrough, he "persevered," became a lawyer and wrote a Pulitzer Prize winning autobiography titled *Fortunate Son: Healing of a Vietnam Vet*, which enabled him to exorcise in part the private devils that had tortured him in war.

In an act recognizing the healing needed in post-Vietnam America, President Ford appointed a nine-member Presidential Clemency Board in September 1974 to rehabilitate the records of those who had less-than-honorable discharges, or who had fled the country to avoid the draft. Lew Puller first provided legal assistance to the board and later served as a full-fledged member. In his moving account of the war, he reflected on the irony that his posture and approach to his responsibility, colored by his experience in combat, oftentimes put him at odds with other members, such as General Lewis W. Walt, USMC (Ret.), one of his father's[47] comrades in arms.[48] His "iron will" failed in the end, and he took his life twenty-seven years after he was so terribly hurt. Perhaps the most fitting memorial to him is the establishment of a center at his William and Mary alma mater, named for him to see that today's veterans receive the benefits to which they are entitled.

Captain F. Breckinridge Montague '66, USN
(Courtesy F. Breckinridge Montague)

Captain Nat Ward IV '60, USA, left a foot in that unhappy place. Lieutenant George Warren, USA, his classmate, also served there, earning a Bronze Star and five Air Medals. He was followed by Lieutenant Colonel Ray Goodhart '61, USA. Lieutenant (Junior Grade) Breck Montague '66, USN, serving on USS *Sioux* (ATF-75), a salvage ship, cleared the wreck of SS *Green Bay*, a merchant ship sunk by underwater swimmers at a pier in Qui Nhon. Sergeant Joe Farrar '65, USA, who was awarded the Silver Star, two Bronze Stars and a Purple Heart, tells us in his oral history of his training as a Special Forces medic and of the general nature of the highly sensitive, still largely classified missions undertaken by him and his fellow soldiers in the Special Operations Group. Only after April 4, 2001, when the command was awarded the Army's Presidential Unit Citation, did some of its missions become public.

John Shaw '62, a U.S. Army photographer, documented the work of the 589th Engineer Battalion in building roads in 1968. His classmate Willis Gregory, a Marine Corps lieutenant, served in the 3rd Reconnaissance Battalion in the same year. Gregory was assigned to C Company of the battalion, which, among other things, observed and reported enemy movement near Khe Sanh at the same time that Bill Dabney and his marines were defending the hill overlooking the base. He left the command just before Christmas Eve 1968, when its members killed a tiger that had killed one marine and attacked another, who was so badly mauled that he later had to be medically retired.[49] Gregory recalled that before his detachment, he had gone on an earlier, unsuccessful tiger hunt and was gratified that the animal, thought to be the tiger that he'd sought, had been killed.

United States obligations in this era were not restricted to Southeast Asia. Master Chief Jesse Hinson '56, USN, served a full thirty years and Lieutenants (Junior Grade) John Hopewell '56, USN, Roger Garlow '57, of the Coast Guard, Murrell McLeod '58, Tom Booth '59, USN, and Sandy Monroe '60, USN, served on various ships, among them USS *Northampton* (CC-1), the National Emergency Command Post Afloat known as the "Great Gray Ghost of the Virginia Coast," destroyers, a minesweeper and a fleet oiler in the Atlantic and Mediterranean. Lieutenant (Junior Grade) Bob McMillan '61, USN, served in Beachmaster Unit Two, embarked on amphibious ships such as USS *Spiegel Grove* (LSD-32) assigned to the Atlantic and Mediterranean Amphibious Ready Groups, and concurrently attained the distinction of serving as an underway officer of the deck for Formation Steaming, as he tells us in his oral history. Tom Fisher '59 served ashore in Coast Guard Headquarters, while Tom McMillan '59 served with the Coast Guard on the Great Lakes. Tom tells us of the thoroughness of his training to be a hospital corpsman and, more importantly, notes what was mentioned before by Hugh Dischinger '41: military service was expected from those who had received the benefits of

Christchurch. It was part of maturing.

Ward "Buck" Scull '61 served in the Army's Medical Service Corps as a captain in a job normally held by lieutenant colonels and was involved in diverse important projects such as formulation and execution of plans for the Walter Reed Hospital building constructed in 1972. His classmate Garland Jefferson entered the Army and served at Fort Sam Houston, Texas, and Fort Monroe, Virginia.

The list of those who served in the Vietnam era goes on and on, unfolding in the Continental United States (CONUS) and overseas, ashore, aboard ships and in the field. Their service, which required considerable leadership ability, had an impact on those with whom they served. Former Petty Officer Richard Reed and his wife offered their condolences to his family when former Lieutenant (Junior Grade) Tom Booth '59, USN, died on December 31, 2011. It was fifty-five years since they had served on the minesweeper USS *Notable* (MSO-460), which played a major role in recovering the nuclear bomb lost off Palomares, Spain, after the collision of a B-52 and a refueling tanker aircraft.

Ensign Robert A. McMillan '61, USN, at Newport, RI, 1966
(Courtesy Robert A. McMillan)

The Vietnam War was to that point a high-water mark of sorts for national involvement in overseas missions that brought forth great divisiveness. Bob Banks '64, a machinist's mate on USNS *J. C. Breckinridge* (AP-167), recalled an instance at the Oakland, California, marine terminal when dissidents attempted to chain themselves to the ship's propeller blades to prevent its sailing. The restraints on the propeller shaft, known as "jacking gear," had been disengaged and only because a Coast Guard patrol boat was nearby was tragic loss of life prevented. The Vietnam War left a nearly indelible mark on our national consciousness, from which it has taken many years to recover.

In many cases, those alumni who served were influenced by faculty and staff who had entered the service, experienced its challenges and knew its benefits. Ed Cox, who served as dean, had sailed on a Coast Guard cutter homeported in Portsmouth, Virginia. Jim Taylor, colloquially known as "Jungle," had been a Motor Machinists Mate, a "motormac," on USS *LST-699*. It was involved in landings at Morotai in the Netherlands East Indies, a base from which our forces could launch air strikes against Japanese forces in the Philippines. After the war, Taylor served aboard USS *Pasadena* (CL-65), a light cruiser on occupation duty. The ship subsequently evacuated civilians from mainland China before it was overwhelmed by Chinese communists. Frederic Riley, a retired Navy captain who commanded the attack transport USS *Monrovia* (APA-31), was a distinguished mathematics teacher. Early in his career he had commanded USS *Sapphire* (PYc-2) a converted patrol yacht whose crew rescued survivors adrift in lifeboats two hundred miles east of Atlantic City, New Jersey, following torpedoing of their freighter SS *Plow City* by the German submarine *U-588*. William Nunn—"the Colonel"—earned a permanent respected place in a generation of alumni and was widely known and feared for his rigorous "white glove" dormitory inspections. Bill Davies had been a navigator in B-25s of the Army Air Force, and Gerry Cooper '53 served in the Norfolk detachment of Helicopter Combat Support Squadron Two (HC2), now known as Helicopter Sea Combat Support Squadron Two (HSC2).[50] Edward Kearney, the school physician who followed Thomas Grove, had been an Army Air Force flight surgeon. Because of the breadth of their experiences and their military service, these men had the ability to show students how to distinguish between the important and insignificant in life; they set an example of honesty and were splendid teachers, giving the students superior preparation for college work. These characteristics, combined with a personal interest in their students, produced friendships that endured long after the teacher-student relationship was ended. They knew, as Hatcher Williams put it, that their students' lives would change dramatically after school and that in many instances the service would play a role in that change. It was a lesson incorporated in his lectures on Michener's landmark tome, *Tales of the South Pacific*. Even those faculty members who had not served saw the value of service and one, "Spud" Parker, arranged for a friend of his to make a presentation at Saturday morning assembly about the opportunities for service in the Naval ROTC program.

The nature and challenge of military service in the last forty years of the twentieth century was profoundly different. Maneuver warfare became less important than responding to guerilla attacks by enemies who often wore no uniforms. In the Navy, for example, the great reliance on circular formations of ships changed, slowly at first. By the end of the century, the armed forces were increasingly engaged to carry out humanitarian missions that relieved human distress by providing proper food and medical care, at home and abroad. The Army provided considerable relief to the victims of hurricane Andrew in Florida and assisted thousands of Haitian migrants who fled their homeland to seek a better life. In an unprecedented but noble operation, a major tent camp was established at the naval base at Guantanamo Bay, Cuba, also known as Gitmo[51] to generations of Navy men who have experienced the rigors of shakedown and refresher training in that place. The camp was brought into being hurriedly so that those who fled their impoverished homeland in often unseaworthy, dangerously overloaded boats and were rescued in the Windward Passage might be cared for and evaluated to determine if they qualified for admission to the United States as asylum seekers. It became clear that only the armed forces had the power to solve certain kinds of problems. Sandy Monroe '60, by then a captain, and John Craine '64, promoted to rear admiral, served there, Sandy writing the official report of the first iteration of the operation and John providing executive leadership and command for the second installment, which not only involved Haitians but also Cubans. Gitmo was clearly a very different place from what they had known as junior officers, when ships and embarked aircraft squadrons spent shakedown and refresher training periods there.

Political figures, such as Senator Bill Nelson of Florida, reinforced the principle above: that only the armed forces had the resources and institutional structure to accomplish such missions. This was further underscored in the military response to Hurricane Katrina, an operation witnessed in part by Lieutenant Meredith Adkins '00, USN, on board USS *Bataan* (LHD-5), a major amphibious ship sent to New Orleans to provide a command and control center from which armed forces personnel brought order to a chaotic, tragic situation when civilian leaders had been unable to do so. In later times, as the threat of the Global War on Terror developed and matured, the function of Gitmo changed dramatically, as we will see.

THE PROTRACTED HANGOVER

The Vietnam War era was a peculiar time for the armed forces, in that President Lyndon B. Johnson attempted to wage two "wars" simultaneously, one overseas in Vietnam, and the other domestically: the so-called War on Poverty, an effort initiated to eradicate social and economic deprivation. The armed forces—in particular the U.S. Army—were directly affected by the linkage of the efforts.

In part this was brought about by a program started by Secretary of Defense Robert S. McNamara, called Project 100,000, a venture in which large numbers of category IV recruits who would have been rejected earlier for mental and physical disability were enlisted. Supporters of the program argued that these individuals were victims of systemic poverty, coupled with racial discrimination, and would benefit from being in the armed forces. Rather than benefitting from enlistment, though, the recruits—known in some quarters as "the moron corps"—served chiefly as battlefield manpower in Vietnam. They were also known as "cannon fodder," and in the end, the experiment was a dismal failure.

The end of the Vietnam War left the U.S. Army badly weakened. In some instances, there was heavy, seemingly endemic drug use. Incidents of assault on those in authority and "fragging," in which hand grenades were thrown into the quarters of officers and non-commissioned officers, had created severe unit cohesion problems. Combat units in Europe had been depleted in strength to provide personnel for Vietnam. As a result of flirting with social engineering and the inconclusive ending to the Vietnam War, the Army became demoralized, and, to some degree, lost its combat effectiveness, its reason for being.[52] Recovering from the stigma of Vietnam required many years.

The years following the stalemate in and ultimate tragic withdrawal from Vietnam were turbulent in American society, and the uncertainty was reflected in the armed forces. Perhaps the tumultuous times were best reflected in the United States Navy, where Chief of Naval Operations Admiral Elmo R. Zumwalt, Jr., USN had brought about deep, dramatic change in an organization sometimes criticized for stuffy adherence to traditional mores and ways of operating. As a lieutenant, Zumwalt, an extremely resourceful officer and 1943 graduate of the U.S. Naval Academy, had commanded a prize crew placed aboard the Japanese ship HIMJS *Ataka* when that ship transited the Whangpoo River to enter Shanghai so that larger U.S. Fleet units that arrived later could avoid Japanese minefields. He rose rapidly in the postwar Navy and became Chief of Naval Operations following a successful tour of duty as Commander Naval Forces Vietnam. Among other things, he issued a series of "Z-grams," directives related to elimination of what were often perceived as needlessly abrasive regulations. These Z-grams dealt with every facet of Navy life, from hair length to the uniforms that could be worn upon leaving ships and stations at the end of the workday. Zumwalt reasoned that only by taking such dramatic action would the "zest of serving at sea" be enhanced, thus improving a dismal retention picture. There were some in the Navy who were strongly critical of Zumwalt, believing that he had weakened if not destroyed discipline in the Navy.

The fleet was shaken as never before by social unrest. There were outright riots on the aircraft carrier USS *Kitty Hawk* (CV-63). Bands of thugs roamed parts of the ship and, in unprovoked attacks, injured other sailors, some quite seriously. In another episode, it became necessary to transfer dissidents ashore from USS *Constellation* (CV-64) to a beach detachment at the Naval Air Station North Island, Coronado, California, so that pre-deployment flight operations on that ship could be conducted. In both cases, the careers of carrier commanding officers thought to have been destined for promotion to flag rank were demolished. In reflecting on the riots, Captain Marland Townsend, the *Kitty Hawk*'s commanding officer during the melees, observed that "the riots had been a real career buster" for him. Similar disturbances rocked the fleet oiler USS *Hassayampa* (AO-146).

Members of Congress, outraged by the spectacle of seeing militant sailors giving "the black power salute" to one another, inveighed against "permissiveness" and "beer and broads in the barracks" and long hair. It was a chaotic, disillusioned time, and some talk circulated that Admiral Zumwalt, who had become a lightning rod and symbol for all that was perceived as bad, would be fired. He kept his job and in time was succeeded as Chief of Naval Operations (CNO) by a series of naval aviators and submarine officers who restored institutional decorum and order, in part by instituting no-nonsense, "zero tolerance" policies with respect to narcotics and alcohol abuse.[53] They sensed the mood in the Congress, if not the country, and it was twenty years before another "blackshoe," as surface officers are known, became CNO again.[54] That officer, Admiral Jeremy M. Boorda, USN, who became CNO in April 1994, was extremely talented and began his career as an enlisted man, rose through enlisted ranks, was commissioned and, through outstanding performance, achieved the rank of full admiral. Boorda, like Zumwalt, was committed to improvement of the welfare of the ordinary sailor. His death by his own hand was a terrible loss, for the Navy and the nation as a whole.

Eventually, however, the armed forces overcame growing pains involving social change and the malaise caused by the debacle in Vietnam. This may have been partially related to the fact that conscription was abolished and pay and allowances were improved markedly. Civilian leadership began the task of rebuilding its sense of pride in the military and did so quickly.

When on May 12, 1975, scarcely two weeks after the fall of Saigon, Khmer Rouge irregular soldiers seized SS *Mayaguez*, an American merchant ship sailing on the open seas in the vicinity of Koh Tang Island, Cambodia, President Ford ordered United States Navy and Marine Corps forces to rescue the distressed sailors, retake the ship and punish those responsible for it seizure. The operation, which was carried out on May 15, 1975, involved USS *Harold Holt* (FF-1074), USS *Henry B. Wilson* (DDG-7), United States Marines and Air Force Special Operations Forces from U-Tapao, Thailand. The operation was a resounding success. The merchant ship was retrieved and towed away by the Holt while marines freed the crew, and air attacks were launched on nearby Khmer Rouge's Ream Airfield, the port of Kompong Som and Khmer Rouge small craft in the vicinity of Koh Tang Island.

The progress toward regaining a sense of national worth and military pride was uneven, and on November 4, 1979, during the Carter Administration, Iranian extremists seized the American Embassy in Tehran and held the staff hostage for 444 days. This humiliating event, combined with a risky attempt to rescue the hostages, known as Operation Eagle Claw, which failed on April 24, 1980, at the cost of eight American lives, in part led to the election of Ronald Reagan as president. On the day of his first inauguration, the hostages were released. President Reagan asserted leadership in a renaissance of the U.S. Armed Forces, and his example clearly influenced the similar efforts of his successors, in particular George H. W. Bush, himself a decorated former naval aviator.

A great part of Ronald Reagan's effort related to his acknowledged skill as the "Great Communicator." He set out to restore pride in the uniformed services in two ways: (1) by using them in novel, yet needed missions, and (2) by using them in traditional roles. For example, in August 1981, after warning he would do so if they did not return to work, he fired striking union air controllers and ordered military air controllers to replace them. Beyond that, he set out to make citizens aware of their heritage and in so doing feel good about themselves and the country, in part by reminding them of the splendid past achievements of members of the armed forces. Nowhere was this done more effectively than in two speeches given in Normandy on the fortieth anniversary of the D-Day landings. In one, he lauded the courage and heroism of those who came ashore through waters tinged with the blood of fallen comrades, including one Robert Zanatta, a former U.S. Army combat engineer whose daughter was in the audience. In another, delivered from a high cliff overlooking the Landing beaches, he reminded us of the gallantry of "the Boys of Pointe du Hoc," those U.S. Army Rangers who, under unremitting enemy fire, scaled the sheer cliffs above the beaches from which he spoke to gain a foothold on the European continent from which the drive to Berlin might be launched.

In the last twenty to twenty-five years of the twentieth century, and particularly as noted above in the Reagan and Bush Administrations, there were many opportunities to reassert American power, diplomatic and military, both in hemispheric and other international matters. In October 1983, led by devoted Marxist Bernard Coard and perhaps ultimately sponsored by Cuban dictator Fidel Castro, forces threatened to overthrow the government of Grenada, a tiny Caribbean nation. More importantly, the safety of one thousand American medical students at Saint George's University was threatened.

On October 25, 1983, U.S. Armed Forces, acting in accordance with President Reagan's orders, carried out Operation Urgent Fury, which not only restored a government untainted by Cuban influence, but also rescued the grateful medical students. Though there was initial stiff resistance from Cuban forces and some Grenadian elements, it collapsed, and President Reagan dismissed the adverse resolution that came from the United Nations[55] and unfavorable comments from Prime Minister Thatcher of the United Kingdom.[56] He was determined to face the threat of communist subversion. His spokesman Larry Speakes observed at a press conference that the U.S. dismissed Cuban and Grenadian assurances that U.S. citizens would be safe because "it was a floating crap game and we didn't know who was in charge." Later an independent congressional investigation found that the invasion was justified, in great measure because of the threat that the students might be taken hostage, as the Americans at the embassy in Tehran had been four years earlier.

Subsequently, on April 15, 1986, in response to a Libyan-sponsored attack on a Berlin nightclub patronized by American servicemen, President Reagan responded with strong operations against the notorious Libyan leader, Colonel Muammar Al-Gaddafi. The action, known as Operation El Dorado Canyon, involved massive air strikes against targets around Benghazi, Tripoli and other installations. Gaddafi's son was killed in one of the strikes. This was an extraordinarily complex evolution. Air Force F-111s from Upper Heyford and Lakenheath in England had to fly over water and be refueled in flight because overflight rights over France and Spain had been withheld by those governments. Other air strikes were mounted from Sixth Fleet aircraft carriers: USS *Saratoga* (CV-60), USS *America* (CV-66), and USS *Coral Sea* (CV-43), also known by the nickname "The Ageless Warrior." This operation was a precursor to subsequent instability and the rising tide of international state-sponsored terrorism. This was given form by the December 21, 1988, Libyan bombing of Pan American World Airways Flight 103, which was en route to the United States over Lockerbie, Scotland, in which all souls on board, including American service personnel travelling on leave and official business, were killed. The atrocity, said to have been personally approved by Gaddafi, not only destroyed the aircraft and those aboard, but also killed eleven citizens and destroyed homes and other properties that were victim to the plane's falling fiery debris.

Presidents used American military power to protect national interests overseas and execute humanitarian assistance projects at home and overseas. For example, from 1984 forward, conflict between Iraq and Iran threatened the flow of vitally important oil from the Arabian Gulf area. Furthermore, on March 17, 1987, the USS *Stark* (FFG-31) was attacked and almost sunk by an Iraqi Mirage aircraft that fired two Exocet missiles that inflicted nearly fatal damage to the ship. Congressional representatives wished to know what our government was trying to accomplish in the Gulf area.[57] Declaring that "use of the vital sea lanes of the Persian Gulf will remain open to navigation by all nations," President Reagan authorized the reflagging of commercial supertankers so that they might be protected by the United States Navy, an operation known as Earnest Will, conducted between July 24, 1987, and September 26, 1988. The Director of Naval History ordered Sandy Monroe '60 to the Joint Task Force Middle East based ashore at Administrative Support Unit Bahrain, and Sandy embarked aboard USS *Dubuque* (LPD-8) and USS *La Salle* (AGF-3) at Manama, Bahrain, to collect material to document this operation. Sandy returned to the Naval Historical Center the flag that had flown on Iran ship *Ajr*, a converted Japanese-built landing ship that was detected and captured while laying mines. He also returned expended 51-mm cartridges collected from her decks before the Navy SEALs who captured and detained the crew scuttled her.

Within the hemisphere, as mentioned earlier, turbulence continued and increased, with the location shifting to Panama. Earlier, President Carter and General Omar Torrijos, who later died under uncertain circumstances, had negotiated turnover of the Panama Canal to that nation. In 1988 and 1989, Manuel Noriega, his successor, presented pressing difficulties. Known to be a narcotics trafficker, the florid, corpulent dictator[58] declared that a state of war existed between the United States and Panama. His so-called "Dignity Battalions" of the PDF (Panamanian Defense Force) harried domestic political opponents. They were involved in the harassment of an American naval officer and his wife, who was threatened with sexual assault, and the murder of a

United States Marine, Lieutenant Robert Paz, in December 1989.

The armed forces had been planning for contingencies in Panama in light of Noriega's increasingly bellicose behavior. On December 20, 1989, President George H. W. Bush ordered execution of Operation Just Cause[59], and, upon securing the removal of the dictator, withdrew forces just after Christmas. President Bush justified the operation as a way of protecting American citizens, removing a known drug trafficker, eliminating domestic human rights abuses in Panama and ensuring the integrity of the Carter/Torrijos agreement turning over the Panama Canal. Noriega, who was temporarily sheltered in the Vatican Embassy, surrendered on January 30, 1990, and was incarcerated in United States federal prisons until April 27, 2010, when he was extradited to France to stand trial on money laundering charges of which he was convicted on July 7 of that year.

Uniformed services have increasingly been used in non-traditional enterprises related to domestic and international hemispheric concerns. From 1989 to this day, the military has been involved in giving assistance to civilian law enforcement agencies (LEAs) as they have tried to eliminate illicit trafficking and consumption of narcotics. Because of the restrictions of the Posse Comitatus Act, the efforts have been restricted to "detection and monitoring" of traffickers to facilitate their "interdiction and apprehension" by civilian LEAs, except in the case of the United States Coast Guard, whose personnel have law and treaty enforcement authority in addition to military responsibilities. The Coast Guard's use of such power and actions are more fully described in the recollections of Lieutenant Ned Burgwyn '04, USCG, of his assignment to CGC *Northland* (WMEC-904), homeported in Portsmouth, Virginia.

Other areas in which the Coast Guard has played a major role and in which all the services have been intermittently involved have been Alien Migrant Interdiction Operations (AMIO), Humanitarian Assistance (HA) and Disaster Relief (DR). Following the ouster in the fall of 1991 of Haitian President Jean-Bertrand Aristide, there was a "mass population exodus"[60] from that unhappy land and, in accordance with existing AMIO agreements, the Coast Guard interdicted the thousands of "economic migrants," as the unfortunate souls were designated by the Immigration and Naturalization Service (INS). They were brought to tent camps established on an inactive airfield at U.S. Naval Base Guantanamo Bay, Cuba, nicknamed Gitmo, where they were given humanitarian care and screened by the INS. The screening was to determine whether those interdicted at sea might be admitted to the United States as "parolees" or "refugees," or instead had to be repatriated to Haiti as "economic migrants." Humanitarian care was left to the armed forces, while screening was done by civilian agencies and one uniformed service, the U.S. Public Health Service.

There were two major efforts: providing humanitarian care and determining eligibility for admission to the United States, for Haitians and later for both Haitians and Cubans, undertaken from 1991–93 and 1994–96. Sandy Monroe '60, a Navy captain assigned to the Joint Task Force GTMO for a time, returned to Atlantic Command Headquarters (USCINCLANT) at Norfolk where he wrote the official history of the first operation. He noted, among other things, that carrying out the humanitarian care mission required patience, adaptability and cultural sensitivity. Haitian migrants would not use military field laundries. The base engineers had to build elevated washstands so that the women could share washing tasks as well as sharing community news and gossip, the custom in Haiti. In addition, in the later stages of the first humanitarian operation, the migrants participated in preparing their meals, which ensured that the food was like what they ate in Haiti.

John Craine '64, by then a rear admiral assigned as Commander Atlantic Fleet Shore Activities, provided executive support for the second humanitarian care/screening operation that was carried on from 1994–96, which involved not merely Haitians but also Cubans. Screening of Cubans was required because President Clinton had decreed that Cubans no longer qualified for automatic admission to the United States as political refugees but had to instead be screened in the same way as Haitians. To this very day, Lieutenant Burgwyn and other men and women of the Coast Guard interdict Haitians, though those interdicted are directly repatriated, and the migrant camps at Gitmo have never been reopened. John Craine '64 reflected on his days at the base, observing that the Haitians invariably arrived on barely seaworthy craft dressed in tattered clothes, while in some cases the Cuban woman balseros, as the rafters were known, might arrive on rafts clutching Gucci handbags. He too recalled situations in which cultural sensitivity was needed. Because there were no sanitary sewers at the base, many port-a-johns were required to accommodate the sudden increase in population, and the migrants were sensitive to the color of the portable toilets.

Unfortunately, aid to Haiti, in this instance given ashore in that poverty-stricken land, was again made necessary following a January 12, 2010, 7.0-scale earthquake. That calamity destroyed the fragile infrastructure in the capital, Port au Prince, and left thousands homeless and living in parks and in the open for fear of aftershocks. USS *Bataan* (LHD-5)[61] played a key role in providing humanitarian assistance, and, in fact, one baby was born on board before the Navy hospital ship USNS *Comfort* (T-AH-20) arrived.

Operation Earnest Will, discussed earlier, a maritime operation, proved a foretaste of more direct robust involvement in affairs in the Persian Gulf for the United States and its allies. Early on the morning of August 2, 1990, mechanized units of the Iraqi Republican Guard invaded Kuwait or, as Iraqi dictator Saddam Hussein called it, "the 19th province of Iraq," assuming control of the oil-rich country. Declaring that "this invasion will not stand," President George H. W. Bush assembled a coalition of thirty partners, known as Operation Desert Storm, to eject the bloody despot. The United Nations passed Resolutions 660 and 662 condemning the invasion and calling upon Saddam Hussein to withdraw, and Resolution 678, setting a deadline for that to happen; and President Bush signed a Presidential Decision directive, outlining United States policy toward Iraq. The coalition was created in large measure by the efforts of President Bush and General Colin Powell, with field command falling to General Norman Schwarzkopf, a stolid, downright West Pointer who was commanding general of the United States Central Command home based at MacDill Air Force Base in Tampa, Florida.

The naked, brutal aggression did not stand due in large measure to the careful assemblage of overwhelming force in accordance with the "Powell Doctrine," and the operation stood down after the Iraqi invaders had been driven from Kuwaiti soil. After about a hundred hours of ground combat, the invading Iraqi Army lay in ruins, with smoldering tanks and other vehicles littering the so-called highway of death, by which they had entered Kuwait at the end of the summer. One witness to the lightning-fast advance toward Baghdad was Lieutenant Colonel (who was then a sergeant and cavalry scout) Mark Vakos '82, who in his oral history recalls his reaction to those events and "roaring across the desert" onward into Iraq.

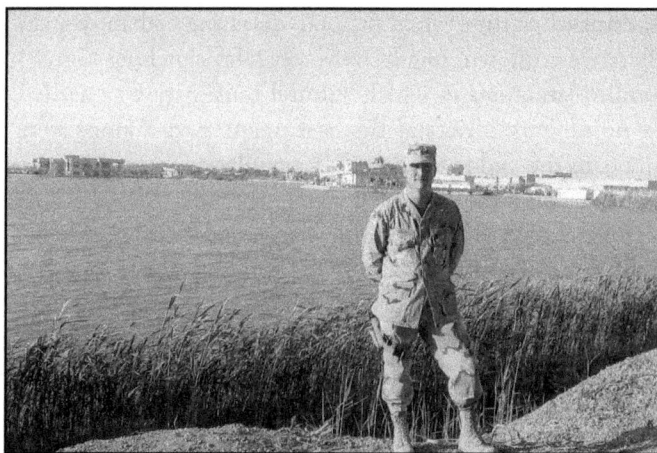

Lieutenant Colonel Mark P. Vakos '82, U.S. Army, near Al Faw Palace in Baghdad, Iraq (Courtesy Mark P. Vakos)

Lieutenant Colonel Boyd Spencer '66 notes in his oral history that he prepared millions of dollars worth of tank ammunition at Fort Knox, Kentucky, for possible use against Saddam Hussein's Republican Guard but was not able to deploy before the war was over. Lieutenant Colonel Gugy Irving '67, USAF, commanded the 354th Base Support Squadron at Myrtle Beach Air Force Base. He was heavily involved in the deployment of combat aircraft to King Fahd International Airport at Dammam, Saudi Arabia, from which they attacked and destroyed Scud missile sites in Operation Desert Shield and provided close air support in the ensuing Operation Desert Storm.

The Middle East, in particular the Persian Gulf area, has proven to be a major source of controversy since Desert Storm ended on March 1, 1991, in the armistice tent at Safwan, Iraq. When that operation ended, there was some frustration that coalition forces had not taken advantage of the initiative, marched to Baghdad and removed Saddam Hussein once and for all. From that time forward, Saddam Hussein and his cohorts proved a chronic irritant, and his activities were augmented by Osama bin Laden and his colleagues. These thugs distorted the tenets of Islam and conducted nearly continuous Jihad against the United States and its allies. Jihad took various forms. These two elements, which were closely related, conducted strikes against a United States billeting facility at the Khobar Towers and attacked and nearly sank USS *Cole* (DDG-67) when she lay at anchor during a fueling stop at Aden. During the entire period from 1991 to 2001, Saddam waged war against the Kurds in Northern Iraq, killing many of them with chemical weapons, and United States forces enforced no-fly zones within the northern and southern regions of Iraq.

Those activities proved vexatious and sorely taxed American logistical capabilities. Though there was some doubt that Saddam Hussein possessed weapons of mass destruction, he used chemical weapons against the indigenous Kurdish population of Northern Iraq. Thus it was thought by many that, left to his own devices, he represented a clear risk to peace in the region.

In the end, coalition forces in the Second Gulf War finished the job, removing Saddam and undertaking a difficult period of reconstruction. Captain Louis Ginn V '04 observed the turbulence as Executive Officer of Apache Troop of the First Squadron of the Third Armored Cavalry. His soldiers provided security so that members of the Karbala Provincial Reconstruction Team could rebuild a badly damaged children's recreation center. While combat forces have been withdrawn, it appears that various "advisory functions" will continue for some time.

The morning of September 11, 2001, was mild, balmy and glorious, full of bright sunshine and promise as millions of New Yorkers went to work, oblivious to the destruction that was about to be rained down upon them. Four aircraft had been hijacked, and two were en route to New York, where they were deliberately crashed into the World Trade Center towers by Islamic terrorists bent on destruction of what they considered to be symbols of unrestrained, corrupt economic power and the unneeded societal excesses of the United States. Millions of Americans watched in disbelief and horror, fixed on the images of death that appeared in real time on television sets nationwide. They were mute, holding their breath and praying for the victims, rescue workers and for the very nation itself. No one can forget where they were on that day, much as many people now alive recall where they were when President Kennedy was assassinated in the late fall, thirty-eight years prior.

Two other commercial airliners were involved in the attack on America. One was crashed into the Pentagon in Washington and the other, thought to be en route to Washington from the Midwest to demolish the capitol building or the White House, was wrested from terrorist control by valiant passengers who forced it down in rural Pennsylvania at the cost of the lives of all on board.

These cataclysmic events forever demolished the fiction of geographic isolation that applied in 1940. The president, who was away from the city, could not immediately return to Washington, and as he flew over the still-burning Pentagon en route to Andrews Air Force Base in nearby suburban Maryland, he reflected that "this is war in the 21st century." In a memorable speech at the Washington Cathedral, delivered in what he termed "the middle hour of our grief," he reminded those gathered there who sought God's hand in the bereavement and smoking ruins that "God's signs are not always the ones we look for." He called the country to unity and arms against a seemingly implacable foe and declared that the struggle would be ended, "in a time of our choosing."

The Summing Up:
A Sense of Place and the Constant River

It was a beautiful river, broad and blue and serene with no cities defacing its shore. There was something primeval about this river: with the woods crowding its shore, its banks and tidal flats and ducks winging southward . . . It seemed as if the river had remained forever changeless, and undisturbed by the tools and weapons of man.[62]

At Christchurch one was always conscious of the natural beauty of the Virginia countryside—of the Rappahannock River, majestic and lazy, flowing away toward the east, and the sound of birds and the beauty of the magnolia trees scattered around the campus. The climate was mild and even on the hottest days there was usually a breeze from the river.[63]

A Form One, according to the book of naval signals, is a formation of ships at sea maneuvering in column where one vessel follows another taking its place and sailing in the wake of the warship just ahead. The long grey hulls are a beautiful sight, gliding one after another through the churning sea, creating a stirring example of the power and grace of the naval service underway.[64]

William Styron, class of 1942, a former Marine Corps lieutenant, and Admiral James Stavridis, U.S. Navy, now commander of United States Forces European Command, have written about continuity and change, which are integral parts of Christchurch School and the Armed Forces experience. Bill Styron tells us of the Rappahannock River,[65] which has, since before recorded time, flowed gently past the high bluff from which generations of boys, and now girls, have watched it. It is bright blue and glistens under the sun in all seasons. It can, however, be grey, cold and forbidding in the bleak midwinter months.

Bob Yarbrough, the legendary ninth headmaster, often called these months "the doldrums" to denote their ennui and power to enervate. When he spoke of the doldrums, he did so to suggest that a new season would follow, bringing with it warmth and restoration, much as spring along the Rappahannock brings the return of the ospreys after their long northward flight.

In all times the river flows inexorably in the manner of tides, and both tranquility and storminess exist along it, just as in our personal lives. The students who gaze down on the Rappahannock can see watermen leave the tributaries in sturdy workboats to earn their livings. The river is a constant. It is a silent force and a reminder of enduring values—honorable labor, goodness, courage, decency, honesty and service to others less fortunate—that have influenced those who have come to maturity along its banks and, in many cases, went on to serve in the armed forces of the United States.

Admiral Stavridis, likewise, speaks in metaphors of continuity and change, key ingredients not only in the Navy but in all of the armed forces, and perhaps in the nation itself, evidenced by the seemingly seamless transitions surrounding deeply moving events of recent times, such as the assassination of President John F. Kennedy. Stavridis does so by describing a "Perfect Form(ation) One," a basic cruising disposition of the fleet set out in Allied Tactical Publication 1 (ATP1), a ponderous document known to and mastered by every underway officer of the deck of a U.S. Navy or Coast Guard ship. It involves a long line of ships, often of varying sizes and classes, proceeding in a straight line in pilot waters or in open ocean at a steady course and speed. They may vary in age, class, type and crew, but they are always there, the ocean opening and closing for each endlessly. They are, in the words of *The 1928 Book of Common Prayer* of the Episcopal Church, "a safeguard to the United States of America and such as those who pass on the seas upon their lawful occasions." Though the admiral focuses on graduates of the U.S. Naval Academy, his essay might as easily describe members of the Christchurch family. Over the years, the line of such individuals has been as steady as the flow of the river or ships sailing in formation. William Robards '27, Miles Libbey '35, Richie Henderson '35 and Fred Riley, a later member of the faculty, are part of the unbroken line of those officers of the deck (OODs).

In his oral history, Breck Montague '66, an OOD himself, describes these individuals as the "Captain's agent," who are responsible for ensuring proper operation and navigation of the ships on which they serve. Surely in more recent days, Bob Montague '52, John Hopewell '56, Roger Garlow '57 of the Coast Guard, Murrell McLeod '58, Tom Booth '59, Sandy Monroe '60, Bob McMillan '61, Breck Montague '66, Meredith Adkins '00 and Ned Burgwyn '04 have learned of Form 1 as they kept watches, in daylight, darkness and stormy, foreboding weather, constantly alert even in seemingly calm times for difficulties that can, and frequently do, emerge unexpectedly to test the mettle and maritime skill of OODs. Breck Montague, for example, had to contend with the unanticipated as he encountered the fury of the sea during Typhoon Kit, when he navigated USS *Sioux* (ATF-75) out of the San Bernardino Strait on a return voyage from Vietnam to San Diego in 1972. The tiny ship, which was made less maneuverable by towing a powerless U.S. Army De Long barge to Hawaii, faced fifty-foot seas driven by hundred-knot winds. Somehow she reached port at Apra Harbor, Guam, undamaged.

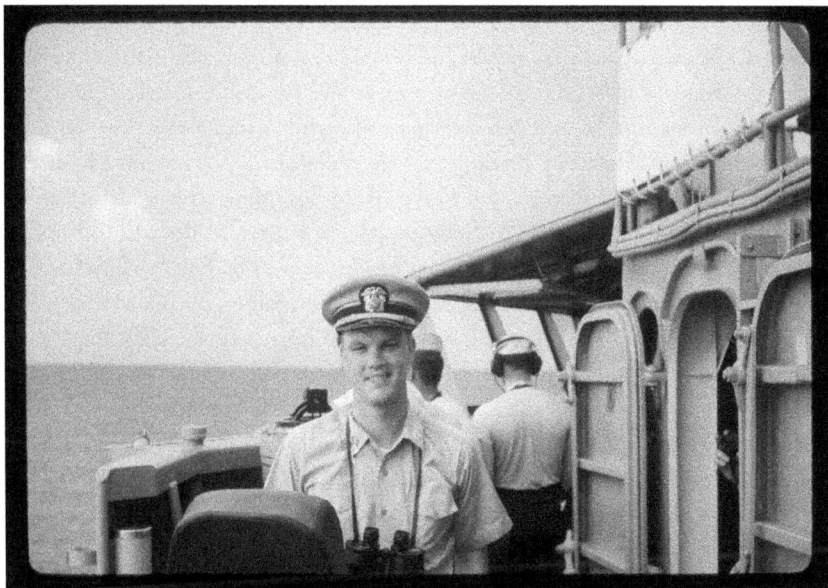

Lieutenant Alexander G. Monroe '60, USN, standing watch aboard USS Henley *(DD-762) at passage from Naval Base Norfolk, Virginia, to Naval Base Roosevelt Roads, Puerto Rico, in 1969 (Courtesy Alexander G. Monroe)*

Those in the other services have met equally difficult challenges. The rigors faced by Captain Sydney Vincent '36 of the Army as he opposed Germans in 1944 were different from those faced by Colonel Bill Dabney '53[66], Lieutenants Nat Ward '60 of the Army and Lewis Puller, Jr., '63 of the Marine Corps, opposing indigenous, often ununiformed Vietnamese insurgents.

In September 2005, Bill Dabney spoke about Vietnam in an oral history conducted at Virginia Military Institute. He felt that because the war was not fought on a peninsula as in the Korean War, because there were no vital national interests involved, and because successful prosecution of the war would entail incursions into Chinese sanctuaries, United States involvement would be defensive in nature. American citizens would tire of it and demand withdrawal of our forces. His brother-in-law, Lewis Puller, Jr., went further. From his perspective as a law student at The College of William and Mary after his retirement from the Marine Corps, he described the national mood, stating that the prevailing attitude was that American involvement in the Vietnam War was, if not downright immoral, certainly a mistake of epic proportions. He concluded that his service had been "meaningless."[67]

Each year in the spring, when green has returned to the trees and the air is gentle, another group of graduates goes forth, as they have every year since 1922, like ships steaming in column. Some, like Thomas Marchant '33 and Richie Henderson '35, are now gone. Tom Marchant returned from war, pursued a successful career, raised his family and now rests in the cemetery down the road from school. He is alongside Bill Jones '28, Everett Blake '32, Taliaferro Bargamin '56 and Bill Bowman '42, who sustained terrible wounds and frostbite in the Battle of the Bulge. Chris Willaford, a Navy veteran who was proprietor of the school store, and Floyd Milby, longtime school maintenance superintendent and former U.S. Navy Seabee, rest there, as does Emmet Hoy, Jr., the chaplain who went on to become headmaster at St. Stephen's School in Alexandria, Virginia. Very recently they have been joined by Bill Dabney '53. Richie Henderson '35 lies under the frequently stormy surface of La Pérouse Strait with his gallant shipmates in the wreck of USS *Wahoo* (SS-238), far from his home in Fredericksburg, Virginia, taken from us before his time. The students leave the hillside above the river and add to an unbroken line that is at once continuous and changing.

Early on, and even in the time of Nat Ward '60, Lew Puller '63 and Willson Craigie '65, it was impossible to imagine that there would one day be female day students at Christchurch, let alone boarders, for adolescent boys were sent there to remove them from the "distractions of the modern city." Yet they are now there, and the school is likely the better for it.[68]

Similarly, since the 1960s, ships and those who sail them have changed in remarkable ways. In 1964, when Murrell McLeod was a lieutenant and assistant engineering officer on USS *Steinaker* (DD-863), and in 1965, when Ensign Bob McMillan was a novice officer in Beachmaster Unit Two, no one could have imagined that women would one day serve at sea, and in fact command combatant ships. Lieutenant (Junior Grade) Johnny Craine, a "nugget" aviator in 1969 who later became a vice admiral, might have been initially shocked but ultimately was likely very pleased to see a female red shirt Aviation Ordnanceman (AO) arming an F-14 Tomcat, or a purple shirt Aviation Boatswains Mate (AB), commonly known as a "grape," fueling an S-3 Viking. Lieutenant Commander Roger Garlow '57 or Lieutenant Ned Burgwyn '04 of the Coast Guard might be less startled, as they have served in a service that introduced mixed-gender crews in its cutters in October 1977.

Ned was, until the summer of 2012, executive officer of CGC *Mustang* (WPB-1316). That ship performs vital search and rescue missions in Alaskan waters. When Ned was detached, it was known that the ship's next commanding officer was slated to be a woman.

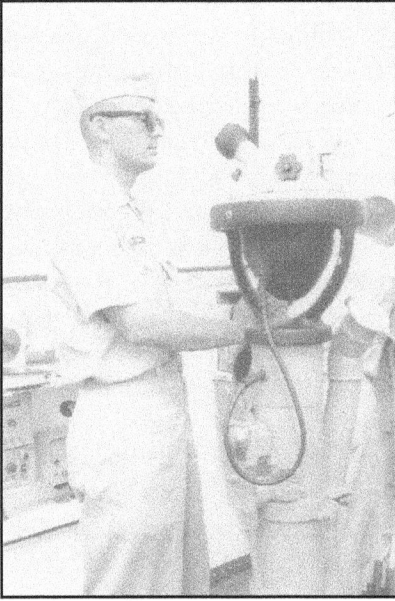

Lieutenant Commander Roger A. Garlow '57, USCG, as an officer candidate at U.S. Coast Guard Training Center, Yorktown, Virginia (Courtesy Roger A. Garlow)

Lieutenant Collinson E. P. Burgwyn III '04, USCG, at Boston, Massachusetts (2012) (Official U.S. Coast Guard photograph)

Change has come, both to the school and to all the armed services, and has gone hand in hand with maintaining tradition as the institutions have participated in pioneering ventures. Lieutenant Meredith Adkins '00, USN, graduated with the class of 2004 at the U.S. Naval Academy and subsequently served in the operations/communications department of USS *Bataan* (LHD-5), a heavy-lift amphibious ship. This ship was commanded by a woman, who would later be promoted to rear admiral. Meredith Adkins, whose educational experience at Annapolis and assignment to a major combatant ship were symbolic of great change in the U.S. Navy, attained the traditional qualification as an underway officer of the deck, as had her fellow male alumni, the lieutenants Montague, Hopewell, Garlow, McLeod, Booth, Monroe, McMillan and those who preceded them.

Even in the Marine Corps, tradition and innovation have gone hand in hand. For instance, the yellow feet on the deck at the Parris Island recruit depot have been seen by generations of new "boots" when they leave the trains and buses that bring them to boot camp. Those feet were seen by Wortie Ferrell '59 and his friend and classmate Jim Newton '59, as well as Jim Enochs '62 when they arrived, and they continue to be seen today.

However, there has been change. One of the more striking examples of innovation has been the career of Major Jennifer Grieves, the first woman to serve as a presidential aircraft commander in Marine Helicopter Squadron One (HMX1), the squadron whose members fly the President of the United States. Her last flight before detaching from the command to attend the Marine Corps Command and Staff College was made with an all-female crew. When queried by a reporter about being the first woman presidential aircraft commander, she said, "It's really not about being a female. It's about being a marine, part of an organization that's exceptional." Likewise, whether male or female, those in the Christchurch family who have served have come from an exceptional organization and have gone on at one time or another to serve in another: the armed forces of the United States, irrespective of branch.

In his biography of William Styron '42, James West focuses on Christchurch and why it served, and still serves, a useful purpose. He holds that many of the students of Styron's day were there because they were "academically lazy" and needed to be energized, a statement with which many would agree. For example, Bob McMillan '61 notes in his oral history that he "simply wasn't applying" himself at Horace Mann Junior High School in Charleston, West Virginia, and that his father felt it was time for him to "buckle down."[69] West goes on to say that Christchurch was a "relaxed" place with an "undemanding schedule," to which many students and former students would take strong exception. They might well concede that they were there to develop regular study habits, that earlier attempts to prepare for college had been less than successful and that the alternatives to Christchurch were undesirable. In some cases, students came from families in which, because of domestic turbulence or absence of a parent, consistent care and discipline were lacking.

Perhaps the best way to observe how the school and the armed forces have been similarly decisive influences in the adolescent development and subsequent adult lives of Christchurch alumni is, as Bob McMillan '61 puts it, to "reflect upon" the oral histories that follow. It's illustrative to think about the Christchurch experience and the military experience in terms of personalities, academic preparation and the overriding environment or milieu, keeping in mind that, in the words of James M. Barrie, the Scottish author of Peter Pan, "God gave us memories so we might have roses in December."

Certain figures appear repeatedly in the printed memories of those who have given oral histories, and in other places. William Smith, fourth headmaster, who was gassed as a soldier in World War I and bore burn marks on his neck, and Robert Yarbrough, ninth headmaster, are larger-than-life figures in the minds of those who have known them. Smith, who saw and felt firsthand the terrible toll of war, was, in the words of William Styron's biographer, an "attitude developer." Hugh Dischinger '41 remembers that Smith was always up to date on events in the world beyond Christchurch, sharing this information at assemblies and "frequently warning us that we could expect to serve in the coming war." It was clear to his students that he deemed military service a key ingredient in the maturation process that should be undertaken by all who were physically fit. One wonders what must have gone through his mind as he prepared young men who would in all likelihood depart for the terrors of World War II, some to return terribly wounded or not at all.

First Lieutenant Hugh C. Dischinger '41,
USAAF, (Courtesy Hugh C. Dischinger)

Robert M. Yarbrough, Jr., was a tall, spare man, known variously as "Bob A" and "the Hawk," who could render even the most voluble candidate for admission mute with a penetrating stare, and who had the unsurpassed ability to extract maximum performance from students and faculty alike. Moreover, he instilled in his charges the notions that "(1) they must be accountable for their actions and that (2) excellence was an end for which all should strive," in the words of Murrell McLeod '58, who won the Bishop's Award for the Class of 1958.[70]

Robert M. Yarbrough, Jr., Ninth Headmaster of Christchurch School
(Courtesy Christchurch School)

Others, such as James C. Taylor, Jr., known as "Jungle Jim" or simply "Jungle," who served aboard a tank landing ship and cruiser in the World War II Navy, are important parts of the school's history. Frederic Riley, a retired U.S. Navy captain and talented mathematics teacher, served on USS *Gunnel* (SS-253), a submarine commanded by Senator John McCain's father. He was, in the words of Breck Montague '66, an "incredibly patient man" with struggling students. Mark Vakos '82 recalls the Reverend Edward M. Gregory, the chaplain who had formerly served as priest in charge of an Episcopal church in the predominantly black, impoverished Church Hill district of Richmond. He recalls that "Pope," as he was known, and Ben Boneventura, dean and later acting headmaster, urged him to "do something with his life." Twelfth headmaster Bob Phipps returned the school to its proper standing after a terrible period of decline. He did so in part by making the benefits of a Christchurch experience available to the underprivileged, something that had never before been done in an organized or significant manner. He was a scholar-athlete, in whose honor the new field house is named, who today devotes a good bit of his time to the school.

The academic course at Christchurch was fashioned to take boys from various backgrounds and immerse them in a rigorous program that would help them overcome their specific academic shortcomings. The overall goal was to establish a uniform level of academic, athletic and leadership performance that would enable students to enter select colleges and universities, and more importantly, to graduate in the standard four years. This oftentimes meant that boys with significant weaknesses were put back to earlier grade levels, a frustrating practice for those who had to do it and one that evokes strong emotions in the recollections that follow.

School life was routine, as students recall, punctuated by such highlights as receiving themes that had been graded by "Jungle," with his numerous and unique red ink marks and comments, written in a "wonderful penmanship." The recollections emerge from interstices of memory with a clarity undiminished by the passage of time. Bob Yarbrough and his Senior Vocabulary is another favorite. It is unlikely that any student in the Yarbrough era will ever forget the distinction between, not among, the words "denotation" and "connotation," or what constitutes an "auspicious occasion." Likewise, none will ever forget his Word of the Day, where he provided not only the definition but the etymology of the word at morning assembly in the study hall of Scott-Taylor. Gugy Irving '67 recalls how the experience of "Senior Vocab," in student patois, enabled him to "hit the ball out of the park" on the Miller Analogies test. The memories vary to some degree among the various masters but in general reflect the devotion, care and concern of the masters. Breck Montague '66 remembers Fred Riley as a superior teacher "who would make sure a kid who didn't get it the first time around got it the second . . ."

The matter of milieu, the environment that has produced leaders at school who went on to be leaders in the armed forces, is perhaps harder to grasp. Boyd Spencer '66 puts it well when he describes the three faculty members who, to him, personified the values of duty and honor—Colonel William Nunn, Captain Fred Riley and Commander (Chaplain Corps) Frank Smart. They taught these values, not through any sort of didactic exercise but rather by personal example. As Boyd Spencer observed, the men he admired the most, already named except for "Rock" Poulson, a track coach reputed to be "tough as nails," were such figures. He notes that "they didn't tell us how to act or dress, they showed us, by personal example." Their lessons were plain: "Gentlemen don't lie, cheat or steal." By extension, in Spencer's mind, "neither do Army officers."

The values learned at Christchurch extended into the military institutions in which young men, and now women, were and are placed in the novel position of having to be accountable for their actions, those of their men and women and the performance of their commands. For underway officers of the deck, it is sobering to know that an improperly executed turn, a missed signal or an incorrectly identified navigational aid at sea might have catastrophic results, such as men's deaths, or grounding or destruction of a ship.

Lieutenant Colonel Gugy A. Irving '67, USAF, Commanding Officer, 354th Base Support Squadron, Myrtle Beach Air Force Base (1991) (Courtesy Gugy A. Irving)

Essential features in the school's surroundings appear in the memories that have emerged. Bob Montague '52 states very clearly, "My experience with boats at Christchurch definitely influenced" his choice of the Navy for military service. It still is a part of his life in his avocation, as he sails his Sailmaster 22D class boat. Further, he has passed along his love of boating and the river to a son who is a national champion in Hampton One sailing class. Bob McMillan '61 tells us that his fascination with the river, as "a boy from the hills of West Virginia," led to him serving in the Navy. Moreover, all those who have contributed oral histories speak of other intangible elements and factors that are harder to grasp and perhaps even more difficult to express.

The single most important feature of the environment was the fact that a person was made accountable for his or her actions, a characteristic common to the school and the armed forces, and a theme stressed in every oral history to follow. Murrell McLeod talks about the hours of detention work, known colloquially as "rockpile," for wiring another boy's desk lamp so that it could be switched on and off remotely after lights out. The purpose was to commit a rule violation in the name of an innocent and bewildered victim by playing to the worst instincts of the overzealous hall monitor who "jumped from radiator to radiator"[71] to catch and upbraid wrongdoers. The joy of such practical jokes was summed up by another former Navy officer, who said, "Christchurch was a discipline I learned to respect, and I am sure I had quite a few hours of rockpile, but I never faced a court-martial or spent any time in the brig." The same anonymous graduate quipped, "I like to tell my wife that she'd have spent half of her time in the brig, for she doesn't obey my orders!"[72]

The milieu of dormitory life could be rough and tumble in the late '50s and early '60s, much like military boot camp, according to Somerville Parker, a much-admired master of those times.[73] It was, in summary, a rite of passage requiring considerable endurance. In a sense, the boys were in a novel environment, with no frames of reference. In nautical parlance, they had no charts, buoys or compasses. They took action and shaped courses slowly, much as is done by a Navy or Coast Guard ship's OOD, who, while proceeding in restricted visibility, hears another restricted visibility signal "apparently forward of the beam."

There were, however, lighter moments. One favorite prank was to stop up the showers so that water would cascade out of the shower room and down the stairs with the force of a waterfall. This seemingly innocuous amusement led to serious warping of the beams of the Bishop Brown, a fact noted by Nelson Williams '61[74] when he and other engineers surveyed the venerable structure to determine whether it could be rebuilt. The lovely red brick walls remain as sturdy as before and evoke strong, wistful memories and a longing for times gone, except in remembrance, where they remain inestimably valuable.

Breck Montague '66 commanded USS *Sioux* (ATF-75), an oceangoing tug on a voyage to Turkey where the ship was to be turned over to that country's Navy. He speaks of what he learned at Christchurch: the necessity of keeping rooms tidy and free of trash and graffiti, "taking ownership" of the spaces where students lived and worked. It is an indispensable aspect of communal life that has obvious application and importance both at school and aboard ship. Some recall waiting on tables in the dining room. Others recall "cubicles"[75] or note the lack of privacy in the communal dormitory showers and lavatories, an aspect only too common in barracks and shipboard life. In the words of one graduate, "You had to learn to share space with other people." As Boyd Spencer put it, your men, for whom you are responsible, eat first. The true leader knows this instinctively.

The "sense of place" that Christchurch and the military services share, an almost ineffable sense of kinship, is well expressed by Meredith Adkins, a young lady in the Class of 2000. She asserts that in both the school and in the Navy, "You are part of a family," with each member expected to do that which is required to get along and reach a certain goal "larger than oneself."[76] Most importantly, she goes a step further, connecting Christchurch of the mid '60s to her time and to the service. According to Boyd Spencer, each new officer comes to the Army "with a clean slate, and makes out of it what he or she wishes to make of it." Meredith speaks of her own senior speech at Christchurch, in which she praised the school as an environment to which students of diverse backgrounds could come and be routinely accepted. Likewise, she contends, in the Navy, it does not make much difference who you are or where you come from as long as you contribute to overall mission accomplishment rather than hindering it. She and others, before and after her, reinforce the truth of John Craine's remark that at Christchurch "you were judged by what you were, not who you were," as it is not simply in the Navy but in all the services.

The school sought and seeks to establish for its students a moral compass that persists beyond time and place. This is the enduring lesson to be learned from those who have watched the strength of the ever-flowing river in their time, and have been heartened by its permanence in their service to the country and subsequent journey through life.

Ensign Meredith D. Adkins '00, USN, at Annapolis, Maryland (Courtesy Meredith D. Adkins)

Captain Hugh C. Dischinger '41
U.S. Army Air Force (World War II)

Hugh Dischinger graduated in May 1941, following his brother Jim Dischinger '39. He began his high school education in the Gloucester County Public Schools and, following two years at Botetourt High School, transferred to Christchurch School. After his graduation, he enrolled in the Class of 1945 at the Virginia Military Institute (VMI). After one and a half years, his formal education was interrupted by active military service in the U.S. Army, first in the Field Artillery and later in the Army Air Corps. He completed flight training and flew the P38 (Lightning) and P39 (Aircobra) aircraft as well as the P47 (Thunderbolt). He was assigned to various fighter squadrons in the Pacific theater of operations, home stationed in Hawaii, Iwo Jima and the Philippines. He was one of a small number of aviators to receive training in the first operational jet fighter, the P80 Shooting Star. Discharged from the Army as a captain, he returned to VMI, earned his degree in civil engineering, attained the credentials of professional engineer and land surveyor, and pursued a highly successful career in professional civil engineering. He contributed to his chosen profession as president of the Virginia Section of the American Society of Civil Engineers and president of the Peninsula Chapter of the Virginia Society of Professional Engineers. He has performed admirable community service as senior warden of Ware Episcopal Church and has earned the Silver Beaver Award of the Boy Scouts of America as well as the St. George Award of the Protestant Episcopal Church. He has served on the board of governors of Christchurch School and the advisory board for Public Utilities of Gloucester County, Virginia.

Coming to Christchurch

My older brother Jim '39 entered at the school in 1937, the recipient of an athletic scholarship, instigated by two members of the local board, the Rev. Dr. Herbert S. Osborn[77] and George C. Cary, a local attorney. Mr. Osborn, rector of our Ware Episcopal Church, was active in the Boy Scouts, had been a semi-pro baseball player and even a cowboy. Cary was an unmarried, well-respected attorney and member of the vestry. Osborn taught us baseball on the front lawn of the Rectory, knocking us fly balls and grounders by the hour. When Jim graduated CS and I had just finished my sophomore year at Botetourt High School in Gloucester, I began my junior year there the next fall, and after several days, my mom announced that I was going to Christchurch School on an athletic scholarship.

Significant influences at school

Mr. William D. Smith, Jr., was the headmaster, and obviously the leader of the faculty. He was a WWI veteran who had been gassed in battle and wore the marks to show it: the back of his neck held the burn marks that could not be hidden by his shirt and coat collars, which he always wore. It being the fall of 1939, he was always up to date on current affairs, and frequently warned us that we could expect to serve in the coming war. Mr. Willis Wills was a small, wiry man who lived on the dorm with us and ran a tight ship. He had been a boxer and no one wanted to challenge him. Mr. Colgan Bryan[78] was a math and science teacher who would brook no nonsense in his classes, which characteristic challenged many of us. One night we hung alarm clocks out our cubicle windows and lowered them to the study hall below, set to go off every fifteen minutes. Mr. Bryan was highly irritated but could do nothing until the chiming stopped. The rest of that night's study hall was very quiet. Of course, all my schoolmates of all the forms [grades] helped me to begin to mature into a responsible student. Some became famous: Vincent Canby, Bill Styron, Langley-Wood, Bill Bowman and Walter Newman among them.

Choosing the armed forces

I was a follower, and whatever my brother did was what I wanted to do. He went off to VMI in the fall of 1939, and I was just starting at CS. Naturally, I would follow him to VMI in the fall of 1941. One's Rat year at VMI is never easy, and neither was mine, but having my big brother there was a real help. I was in D Company at VMI, a field artillery ROTC company. When war came that year, at VMI we were placed in the Enlisted Reserve. We learned to ride the horses and pull the caissons at parade—sometimes a hazard when your horses were headed straight for the barracks and you had a hard time turning them. In the fall semester of my third class [sophomore] year, the Army Air Corps sent a team to the Institute looking for prospective pilots. I reasoned that it would be better to be soaring above than slogging in the mud below, and I applied. I passed all the requirements and was transferred to the Army Air Corps Reserve. The transfer came through on February 7, 1943, and I got orders to report for duty on February 17, 1943, a few weeks before my nineteenth birthday. Tough duty—I went for basic training to Miami Beach, Florida, and practiced close order drill marching up and down the golf courses and sleeping in a luxury hotel.

Service history in the military

The Air Corps flight training schools were backed up with too many students, and so we were assigned to colleges around the country to study fourth-grade math and sixth-grade English and to march around the towns a lot. I went to Wittenberg College (now university) in Springfield, Ohio. My father, a construction engineer, was the resident engineer for the electric power station being built there, and my older brother Irvin also worked there, so I got to go out to dinner often.

After a couple of months in Springfield, my squadron was sent to Santa Ana, California, for pre-flight training and then to Santa Maria, California, for primary flight training in Stearman biplanes. From there, I went north to Chico, California, basic flight training and then to Luke Field at Phoenix, Arizona, for advanced training, where I got my wings as a fighter pilot. While at Luke, we had the opportunity to get a few flight hours in the famed P-40.

I had forty-eight hours at home, after fifteen months in training, travelling from Phoenix to Richmond and then to Salinas, California, a pilot pool station via railroad day coach. I then travelled up the West Coast to Washington State and then east out in the desert to Moses Lake, not far from Hanford, where nuclear bombs were being built. Of course, we didn't know that and only found out later. We transitioned into the P-39 Aircobras and P-38s there. Our instructors had flown them in combat . . . mostly in the Southwest Pacific theater.

It was at Moses Lake that we were formed into a supposedly secret group, one of the five termed VLR [very long range] groups training to escort B-29s to Japan from bases that had not yet been taken. We became the 508th Fighter Group, and I was in the 468th Fighter Squadron of that group. There was some indecision about what type planes we would fly, and so we were sent to Bruning, Nebraska, to transition into the P-47 Thunderbolt.

Our port of embarkation was Seattle . . . aboard the Queen of the Matson Lines, the SS *Matsonia*, a luxury liner, at midnight, December 31, 1944. Also aboard was the first contingent of Navy WAVES [Women Accepted for Volunteer Emergency Service] to be deployed to the Pacific bound for Pearl Harbor. Of course we were segregated from the WAVES! Our group expected to deploy from Hawaii to combat as soon as our new base was secured by the Marines—I have the utmost admiration for those Marines. I cannot believe the action they had at Iwo Jima, nor how they accomplished their magnificent victory. In the interim, our job was to patrol the Hawaiian Islands to identify incoming aircraft—fun but useless, as I found many assignments in the military are.

After several months of frustration, we learned that the commanding general of the 7th Fighter Command to which we were attached would not turn us loose. We were the first fighter group he had had in his command since Pearl Harbor and he was not about to let us go anywhere. As a consequence, we began to volunteer individually to transfer to combat units. I had just gotten my silver bar as a 1st lieutenant when he finally cut me loose, and I went to Iwo Jima via Saipan. I was attached to the 413th Fighter Squadron of the 414th Fighter Group flying P-47Ns, the only one with an automatic cruise control system similar to those bombers used.

It was late in the war. I didn't have time to build up a combat record and increase the number of "points" required for separation right after the war ended. I had flown P-51 Mustangs in Hawaii, so I was transferred back and forth between P-47 and P-51 squadrons to replace high-point pilots leaving for home. While at Iwo, I had two accidents. I like to tell people that I have two planes to my credit—both ours. The first occurred at about 6,000 feet above the island. Another P-51 flew into our flight of four P-51s and hit three of us. Our flight leader took the greatest blow and he and the pilot of the plane that hit us bailed out and parachuted successfully. I was hit by flying debris and it knocked out my engine. I had to decide whether to bail out or land dead stick. I decided on the latter and landed downwind but without further damage. The official report lists me as LAS [lost at sea]. I found that out recently and requested that the record be corrected!

The second accident was an engine failure on takeoff in a P-47. We were leaving Iwo for our new assignment at Clark Field in the Philippines. My wingman and I were halfway down the runway when my engine conked [out]. SOP [Standard Operating Procedure] was to drop the external wing tanks, pull up wheels and belly land. I decided I couldn't do that, because I'd have dropped the wing tanks right in front of my wingman and we'd have two wrecked aircraft instead of one. He finally got by me. I tried to do the rest, but I had too much speed and crashed off the end of the runway. Friction caught the internal wing tanks on fire but I got out without a scratch.

We flew from Clark Field for a while and then moved to a Japanese fighter strip south of Clark in the middle of the desert with no trees, living in tents again. We had no buildings and decided to take down some surplus Quonset huts at Subic Bay, transport them to our base and reassemble them. Someone found out I had had a year of engineering training, and so I was put in charge. I had a squad of Japanese prisoners to do the labor, and I could converse a little with the squad leader. These people had not been home in seven years, first fighting in China, and then moving down the island chain to Luzon. I told the squad leader all kinds of lies about the abilities of our planes, and they were obviously impressed. I often wonder what those same people think of what I told them.

My squadron was selected to receive the first operational jet fighter, the P-80 Shooting Star. I was ranking flight leader—the third to check out after the squadron commander and operations officer. We had no dual flight instruction since it was a single seat aircraft. We were given twelve hours of ground training, got in and pushed the "go handle." [It was] a great thrill, cruising at about double the speed of the planes we had been flying. Once I was invited to buzz the field. [I] went down the runway about ten feet up and was clocking 550 mph when I passed the control tower, and that was about sixty-five years ago. The squadron commander wanted me to stay in the service, go back to Arizona for training and then return to the squadron as a jet instructor. The scuttlebutt was that one couldn't retain his commission without two years of college. I had only a year and a half, so I turned him down to return and get my degree in civil engineering from VMI. I was promoted to captain, separated from the service at Fort Bragg, North Carolina, and became a reservist again at age twenty-two. Later I was assigned to the Air Force Reserve but saw no more active duty.

Communal living at Christchurch and in the military

Communal living was never a problem for me. From what I have said above, you can see that I lived and enjoyed a structured life.

The Christchurch experience and military life

In the military people around me were much more diverse, and I saw a few bad ones. At Christchurch, we were all boys growing up, and I developed some leadership qualities as a counselor and in sports. I lettered in football, basketball, baseball and track. I know something about sailing, having grown up in Gloucester, and enjoyed the Hampton Ones we sailed in the spring and spent all winter repairing. I enjoyed military life and was class agent for my Brother Rat Class of 1945 at VMI [Virginia Military Institute], although I didn't graduate until January 1950. One of my roommates was General Sam Walker, son of General Walton Walker and personal friend of General George S. Patton, Jr. Sam was the youngest man in our class coming to Lexington from Indio, California, where he had been on maneuvers with his dad and Patton during the summer of '41. Sam spent a year and a half at VMI and transferred to West Point, as his dad and Patton had done, graduating in the class of 1946. He retired from the Army with four stars and spent a term as superintendent of VMI. He new lives in Pinehurst, North Carolina.

On the observation by Vice Admiral John W. Craine, Jr., '64, USN (Ret.), that at Christchurch and in the armed forces, one is judged not "by who you are but what you are."

John is right, although I served in the Air Corps with a group of vastly different backgrounds and ethics. If you were a good flier, little attention was paid to your ethics. Both Christchurch and VMI taught me differently.

Commander Robert L. Montague III '52
U. S. Navy (Cold War era)

Robert Montague, son of a career officer of the United States Marine Corps who had been decorated with the Navy Cross for extraordinary heroism in World War I, was a day student during the session 1946–1947. Though there for but a short time, he amassed a fine record as a student and learned the skill of being a fine sailor in the school's Hampton One Fleet. These are skills of a lifelong avocation that he has since passed on to his son. He earned a Bachelor of Arts degree at the University of Virginia. Commissioned through the Naval Reserve Officers' Training Corps, he served ashore at the Naval Academy Preparatory School and afloat in all departments on USS *Corry* (DDR-817), a radar picket destroyer home-ported in Norfolk, Virginia.[79]

Coming to Christchurch

I came to Christchurch in 1946–47 because my parents, Brigadier General and Mrs. Robert Latane Montague, settled in Urbanna, Virginia, upon my father's return from fighting the Japanese on Saipan, Tinian [Marianas Islands] and Okinawa during World War II. He retired from a thirty-year career in the Marine Corps at that time.

Significant influences at school

The significant figures at school who most influenced my development were Robert Bailey and James Ratcliff.[80] Mr. Bailey was my science teacher and also taught me how to sail in the Hamptons on the Christchurch waterfront during summer camp and during the school year. He did a grand job of both, as I eventually went on to become a biology assistant at the University of Virginia . . . , partially because of the excellent groundwork he laid for me, and helped pay may way through college that way. I am still sailing frequently to this day in a Sailmaster 22(D) and have a son I taught to sail and steered to the Hampton Class of One Design sailboats. He is now a five-time national champion of the Hampton Class and will be defending his title this coming August. My interest in the Hampton Class is directly traceable to Bob Bailey.

James Ratcliff was the headmaster of Christchurch School during the year 1946–47 that I attended. He was an excellent headmaster and motivated me to become the student who had the highest grade average in the entire school during my year there, for which I won a prize at commencement exercises. My parents moved to Texarkana, Texas, after my year at Christchurch [where] I attended Texarkana Junior High School. I was again the number one boy student in my ninth grade class. I went on to graduate from Episcopal High School in Alexandria, Virginia, in 1952 and the groundwork laid in my prior schools served me well there.

Choosing the armed forces

I joined the Navy because my father had been a career marine who had started as a private in World War I, won a Navy Cross and a battlefield commission and, after coming home and finishing college at the University of Virginia, decided to accept a regular commission. He insisted that I should try to enroll in a program that would lead to a commission and left it up to me to choose which service I preferred. I was accepted into the Naval ROTC [Naval Reserve Officers Training Corps] at the University of Virginia, where I graduated in 1956 with a commission as an ensign, U.S. Naval Reserve.[81] My experience with boats at Christchurch School influenced my preference for the Navy and my parents supported the choice. Besides my father, I had ancestors who fought in the Civil War for the Confederacy and in the American Revolution. My Revolutionary War ancestor was a naval officer on whose account I am a member of the Virginia Society of the Cincinnati.

Service history in the military

I had two duty assignments while serving on active duty from 1956–58. The first was teaching American History and coaching wrestling at the Naval Academy Preparatory School [NAPS] at Bainbridge, Maryland.

The second tour was spent aboard USS *Corry* [DDR-817]. In thirteen months aboard that ship I served in every department except supply and was qualified as an officer of the deck underway. I did cruises to the North Atlantic above the Arctic Circle, the Mediterranean and the Caribbean and became acting engineering officer despite being a history major in college. I matured more in my time on that destroyer than in any other year of my life. My shifts through the various departments happened because of the physical illness of one officer who had to be transferred ashore to a hospital, and another officer who had a nervous breakdown trying to take on the job of the hospitalized officer and wound up being retired from the Navy for mental illness.

As a result of my shipboard experience, I decided to stay in the Ready Reserve, retiring as a commander in 1979 after twenty-three years service. I became executive officer of a large surface division in Alexandria, Virginia, but did not get the opportunity to be a commanding officer because the program was abolished at the end of the year in which I was executive officer. The closest I came to command was as area coordinator of the Blue and Gold program for screening and recruiting [candidates] for the Naval Academy. I wound up my career in the Naval Reserve in the Naval Sea Systems Command in Crystal City. I did not serve on active duty during wartime, but I took the chance of having to do so, so I had a number of interesting and enjoyable two-week ACDUTRAs [Active Duty for Training periods] aboard an aircraft carrier, an oiler and a DE [Destroyer Escort] and [at] places like Newport, Rhode Island, Key West, Florida, Kansas City, Annapolis, Maryland, and at the Pentagon and Washington Navy Yard.

While there is some danger in Navy service, my active service was in peacetime, for which I am thankful. My only injury while on active duty was having my nose broken while coaching the heavyweight wrestlers at NAPS. I had an opportunity to do many things as a young naval officer that were difficult at times and entailed greater responsibilities than I might have had elsewhere. I had an encounter with the service of gay personnel in the Navy that convinced me that they could be effective naval officers. This situation had something to do with my shuffle through various departments of the ship that made my active duty service much more of a challenge than it might have been.

On the observation by Vice Admiral John W. Craine, Jr., '64, USN (Ret.), that at Christchurch and in the armed forces you are judged not by "who you are but by what you are"

John Craine is partially correct, but both who you are and what you are are important. Not all people are alike, and being in the Navy exposed me to a wide variety of humanity that a somewhat sheltered upbringing did not confront me with.

COLONEL WILLIAM H. DABNEY '53
U.S. MARINE CORPS (Cold War/Vietnam era)

Bill Dabney, who was born in Canada and grew up in Costa Rica and Panama, entered Christchurch from Gloucester County, Virginia. He was a student leader, evidenced by his service as a monitor and in other responsible assignments on campus. Upon graduation, he matriculated at Yale University, and following one year in New Haven, enlisted in the United States Marine Corps. Following his release from active duty, he enrolled in the Virginia Military Institute and concurrently served in the Marine Corps Reserve. Following his June 1961 graduation from the institute, he was commissioned a 2nd lieutenant and resumed active duty. He served in a variety of assignments, with the Fleet Marine Force, ashore at Naval Base Rota Spain and with India Company, 26th Marines, in the Republic of Vietnam. During two tours in Vietnam, he earned two Bronze Stars, a Silver Star, and the Navy Cross for conspicuous gallantry and intrepidity. His performance in shore duty was equally strong, in such diverse assignments as operations officer in the Airborne Command Post of the Strategic Air Command at Offutt Air Force Base, Nebraska. His final assignment as commanding officer of the NROTC Unit at his Virginia Military Institute alma mater was unique, and, in fact, unprecedented, in that he concurrently served as commandant of cadets.

Coming to Christchurch

I came to Christchurch circuitously. My father was in the employ of General Motors Export Corporation. He met Mother at St. John's, Newfoundland, Canada. When it came time to give birth to me, that's where she went, so that's where I was born. Because of father's work, we lived in Hawaii, Cleveland, New York and then Costa Rica and then Panama.

I mention the last two, Costa Rica and Panama, because they were, if not unique, at least unusual educational experiences. We got to Costa Rica in 1939, at which time I was five years old. It was decided by my parents to pack me off to kindergarten. The only one in San Jose was German, and I apparently did fine until my mother's birthday. I came home, clicked my heels sharply and said "Happy Birthday, Mother. Heil Hitler!" Obviously, I never went back to that kindergarten, and when my parents went storming down to investigate what was going on, they of course challenged the director who said, "Look, all educational policy in the German nation is dictated from Berlin. Since all funds come from Berlin, I have no choice but to adhere to the policies dictated. The policy requires me to indoctrinate the young men into the Hitler Youth." I still remember some of the songs and a few things like that but not much. I think you probably can understand from whence came my lifelong aversion to the federal government's being involved in education. I was pulled out of the kindergarten, and very shortly thereafter we moved to Panama. There I spent five years at the Spanish Jesuit School. Civilian Monks and Jesuit Monks taught there. I don't remember that part of my schooling pleasantly, because I was the only gringo in a Spanish school. Having said that, the education was superb. I had finished decimals and fractions by the third grade. I could read, write and speak English and Spanish fluently. You were simply told what you were expected to learn. The last year in Panama I went to Canal Zone public schools. They were American schools.

I came back to Virginia in 1946. I first matriculated at the Gloucester County public schools. I think I flunked every course I took. I was bored stiff, but since I didn't cause any trouble, I was ignored. Gloucester schools in those days were designed for farmers and fishermen. So I spent two years at Christ School and two years at Christchurch, grades ten and twelve.

Goals in coming to school

I don't think I gave it much of a thought, frankly. I was fourteen, fifteen, something like that. It was just where they sent me. You don't have objectives and stuff at that age. You just sort of move from day to day. At least, I didn't have any burning desire for any particular thing. I was, in Gloucester County where I lived, right on the water, the North River. I was totally comfortable in the water, to the point that when I got to Christchurch, I took over the waterfront duties—the boats, the pool and all that. I remember getting up at 3:00 in the morning, getting in the school carryall and driving down and turning the pumps on to get the pool filled and that sort of thing.

The school infrastructure and reaction to it

There was an above-ground swimming pool. One of the problems was that it was salt water, and that meant when you pumped it full, you pumped in everything, including the barnacles and mussels and everything else. So about every week you had to drain the darn thing and scrape all the walls because otherwise you would cut yourself to ribbons.

The gym and the cubicles were there, and that is what you got. After my first year there, I was a monitor, and so I had a room—myself and Carl Barnes. We roomed together. Remember that I had been in German kindergarten in Costa Rica and an air raid shelter in the Canal Zone. I thought, all right, this is what I have.

The "workjob" experience

Again, I and a fellow named Clem Holladay[82] were the two big boys in school. I mean, I was six-foot-four and weighed 192 pounds, and let me tell you, in 1953 six-foot-four was a big guy. It's not a big guy now, but it was then. So, Clem was a farmer, and between us we pretty much took care of the tractor, we took care of the waterfront and the boats and stuff like that. We had the skills that we used in that respect. So I didn't do a lot of digging ditches and that sort of thing. I had enough skills so I was in charge of something. I was probably the best vehicle driver there. I had done a lot of driving on farms in the summertime. So I drove the school bus and carryall when we went on trips. I was always, as I remember, the designated driver. I remember once driving up to Valley Forge, Pennsylvania, for a debating contest, and regularly we would drive to Richmond for concerts at the Mosque and mixers with St. Catherine's.

The athletic experience at school

I never played football in Panama. In Panama it is too hot to play football. You would die if you put football togs on. It's just too hot. So initially I did not play football at Christchurch. Then a fellow named Ward Littlefield,[83] who was a running back, a good friend, got pretty seriously hurt playing ball. I remember it caved in his cheekbone, and we used to have to tie him to his bed so he wouldn't roll over and put pressure on it as he was healing. Well, you have got to remember there were only thirteen in our senior class, so getting a football team together was quite a trick. So I said, Ward can't play, so I'll play. I played in his place. You know, I didn't know anything about football. It was only my senior year. I guess I was effective, in that I was big and strong and in good shape. I wasn't particularly quick. I could run forever, but it took me some time to build up speed. Long, lanky guys are usually very good at football because you don't need to be strong and fast, but you need to be strong and quick, and I wasn't quick, and I still am not. I played basketball—not very well—because I was tall. Again, Christ School didn't have a gym either in those days, which meant they didn't play basketball. That meant that when I got to Christchurch, it was the first time I had ever seen a basketball.

Having said that, my physical fitness was good. You are talking about a guy who had spent summers working on a dairy farm. I could swing an eighty-pound bale of hay like you wouldn't believe. I remember one day just after I got to Christchurch and somebody was playing around and somebody challenged me to do a sort of handstand and swing rope. They said, go up the rope and touch the top bar. I grabbed the rope on each side and just pulled myself up, not using my legs at all. I was in pretty good shape.

When it came to Orange and Blue Day—I don't know if they had that when you were there. They split the school into halves, and there was a big competition to see which one won. I remember one of the things was about a six-mile run through the Barnhardt farm [the duck farm], a pretty good run, probably six miles. We ran down to the bridge into Urbanna and back. When I finished, [I was] probably a good half-mile ahead of the next one. It wasn't a problem. I am not talking about condition. I just wasn't athletically inclined.

Communal living at school and in the military

Well, first remember that I didn't start at VMI. I started at Yale. I got lost at Yale. Yale was impersonal. To this day I have difficulty recalling any member of the faculty or administration. I have some friends from there . . . , they were fine lawyers . . . I don't remember anyone's paying any attention to me. At Christchurch, you were always someone's concern. You remembered everybody and related in some way to all hands.

My father had been an ensign in World War I, and when World War II came along, he volunteered his services as an engineer. He was quite a mechanical engineer by vocation. Anyhow, so that last year we lived at the 16th Naval District Headquarters in 1945 in the Canal Zone, right at the Pacific entrance to the Canal.

Panama, because of what was required to build the canal, spurred tropical medicine along and since there were considerable medical challenges from the Pacific—dengue fever, malaria, etc.—a lot of the troops that got sick in places like Guadalcanal, New Guinea and New Britain, were sent back to Panama because they could be treated there. Most of those were marines. There were a lot of marines around. As they were recovering, they'd do things like gate duty and so on. I am the CO's [commanding officer's] son, and I have the run of the station and my own bicycle. I got to know some of the marines pretty well, and they were away from home and they adopted me. I left Panama with a very pleasant memory and association with the United States Marine Corps. Also, when the war ended, we used to take the crash boats up at the naval station and go deep-sea fishing. I discovered I got seasick.

So when I did not succeed at Yale—that is a euphemism for flunked out I guess—I decided I needed self-discipline. I didn't want to go to a jerkwater college and just make up the time there. I needed to do something else. I naturally gravitated to the Marine Corps. Now it didn't occur to me that if I was going to join the armed forces that there would be a better place than the Marine Corps. What I was wanting was something I had found at Christchurch, which was to find such a group of competent, dedicated men in leadership positions who were sincerely devoted to their cause. Christchurch had that in the faculty, and the Marine Corps had it. Christ School had it, too. I was impressed that these people cared about what they did and they put their hearts into it.

On the observation by Vice Admiral John W. Craine, Jr., '64, USN (Ret.), that at Christchurch and in the armed forces you were judged not "by who you are but by what you are"

Positively, I think he's right. I don't remember anyone knowing or caring what you came from, at either place, Christchurch or the Marine Corps. There was unremitting discrimination in the Marine Corps, based exclusively on performance. It comes back to the idea that these guys were dedicated to their job, both the masters at Christchurch and, somewhat to my surprise, the officers and senior non-commissioned officers in the Marine Corps. They cared.

Tone, ambience and values at school

We pulled stuff on each other, but it's nothing that was organized or malicious or anything like that. I don't remember much. Once I became a monitor, I had to stand above that a little bit, just for appearance's sake. Generally speaking, we got along well. I don't remember any feuds. It was an exceptional, eclectic student body. We had preachers' sons and farmers' sons and fishermen's sons and businessmen's sons—you name it. Everybody was sort of mixed in together, and each class was so small, there was no possibility of cliques. When you have thirteen people in a class, it is hard to have a clique. We just got along. Christchurch offered you the opportunity to get away now and then. We were allowed to keep shotguns and hunt on that land behind the church. We hunted regularly, not often. Three or four times during squirrel season I'd check my shotgun out and go. I guess one of the masters stored it for me, as I remember. Not many schools in the world would allow you to take a shotgun to school.

The abiding value of the school

I think in terms of what it did for me. It increased some sense of responsibility. I was always responsible for certain things, like getting the debating team to Valley Forge or keeping the pool filled or getting the grass cut or whatever.

School leadership and religious ritual

Bob Yarbrough was new, and he was just a master and a good one. I don't remember any leadership ability. We did all that with Branch Spalding. I thought and think to this day that we were allowed to govern ourselves. Monitors really had some power, I mean, within limits. You could actually enforce the school's codes and regulations. The honor council had some bounds. I recall being involved in a dismissal, a young lad who had been guilty of cheating in class. Being at that point, that Branch Spalding would allow the honor council to function and [would] receive our recommendations on such a weighty matter as dismissal of a boy, was a lot.

I liked the ritual. The whole school was ritual, but it was mainly the religious ritual. It gave a sense of regularity, permanence and anchor. It was found in matters such as morning and evening prayer, and the Sunday service, which was always at Christ Church. Our auditorium, you understand, was the parish hall, for the school didn't have its own auditorium. For graduation we put chairs in the gym, but there wasn't an auditorium as such.

Master Chief Navy Counselor Jesse L. Hinson '56
U.S. Navy (Cold War/Vietnam era)

Master Chief Jesse Hinson, U.S. Navy, was an accomplished athlete at Christchurch School, evidenced by a four-year membership in the Monogram Club, serving as co-captain of the varsity football team and earning the Dick McDonough Award as Best All-Around Athlete in his senior year. In February 1957, he enlisted in the United States Navy. He began his career as an illustrator/draftsman and later converted to Navy Counselor, retiring after some thirty years of service. His career included such diverse assignments as Mobile Construction Battalion Seven, USS *Northampton* (CC-1), which was the alternate National Emergency Command Post-Afloat (NECPA),[84] USS *Newport News* (CA-148) and Operational Test and Evaluation Force (OPTEVFOR). He retired as a Master Chief Navy Counselor.

Coming to Christchurch

Well, my dad built Headmaster Spalding's cottage over in Weems during the summer of 1952, and Mr. Spalding asked my dad if I would like to come to Christchurch, and my dad answered, "I am not sure, why don't you ask him?" And so he did, and I said, "Sure, I'd like the opportunity." That's how I ended up here at Christchurch. I was a full-time boarder. I ended up getting an athletic scholarship, which defrayed some of the expenses and was the main reason I got a chance to come to Christchurch, to be perfectly honest.

Significant influences at school

Well, obviously Branch Spalding being the headmaster was a direct influence because he was the first point of contact. Being an athlete, I bonded pretty well with all the coaches. Dick Working was the first, Hatcher Williams was number two, Grover Jones was three; and playing multiple sports, I won't go through and name all the coaches, but they had a major influence. Emmett Hoy, who was the parish preacher, had a direct influence on my behavior. I had a tendency to spend too much time on the athletic field and not enough in the classroom, the academic part. He gave me an analogy that has lasted all of my life. He said, "Jess, you have to be sincere; it is like talking on the telephone. If you are sincere, you get an answer. If you are insincere, you get a busy signal." I've kept that philosophy to this very day. I really thought a lot of Reverend Mr. Hoy.

Choosing the armed forces

Growing up in White Stone and living on the water, and my dad was a contractor mostly during the summer months, and in the winter we oystered and we fished crab pots during the summer and being around the water—it just seemed natural that if I joined the service, the Navy would be the one that I would join. But it is ironic because on February 28, 1957, a Navy recruiter stopped on the side of the road and my dad and I were putting an asphalt-shingle roof on a house, and he asked me if I knew a young man named Sonny Jones who happened to live in White Stone, and I said sure. He said he'd shown an interest in joining the Navy. I took my nail apron off, looked my dad in the eye and said, "Tell mom I won't be home for dinner." I got in the Navy car, put White Stone, Virginia, in the rear-view mirror, spent thirty years in the Navy and enjoyed every moment of it. The Navy was good to me, for me and I have no regrets.

Service history in the military

I went to boot camp at Bainbridge, Maryland, and then to Draftsman A School at Oxnard, California, followed by CIC [Combat Information Center] School at Glynco, Georgia. A year later, I went to Mobile Construction Battalion Seven, where my duty involved building a Coast Guard LORAN Station on Grand Turk Island. From there I went aboard USS *Northampton* [CC-1], the USS *Newport News* [CA-148], and USS *Little Rock* [CLG-4]. After I completed those tours, I went to the staff of Chief of Naval Air Basic Training at Pensacola, where I spent five years, a great tour. I went from there to the USS *Sperry* [AS-12], a submarine tender in San Diego, and then returned to Norfolk to Operational Test and Evaluation Force [OPTEVFOR], a very good duty station, the Navy's Ralph Nader organization for all Navy products and services. We inspected everything from chewing gum to women's underwear. It was a very interesting time.

Captain Slade Cutter and Christchurch School

Captain [Slade] Cutter[85] was probably one of the most knowledgeable Navy men I've ever had the privilege to serve under. He was a real man. We sat off the VACAPES [Virginia Capes] after being at sea about a month and called port services to get a harbor pilot, and four hours later, the harbor pilot had not shown up, so Captain Cutter said, "All ahead 1/3, we're going into port." As we neared the pier, the port pilot radioed for permission to come aboard and he radioed back permission denied—"the Navy spent a lot of money sending me to boat driving school, by God, and I'm going to take her to the pier," and he did. I won't ever forget that man. He was the man as far as I was concerned.

Communal living at Christchurch and in the military

In actuality, it prepared me pretty well, for we had communal living—the showers with the bathrooms. It is the same on a ship. There is no difference. Obviously on board ship, you have a whole lot less room. You've got twenty square feet on a ship compared to a hundred square feet here at Christchurch. It is just compacted. The discipline—at Christchurch—I was a little bit rank. I spent a lot of time on rockpile. Eli Carter, who was the maintenance man, gave me a paintbrush, and I think I painted everything on this campus that didn't move. As far as discipline in the service, I think I was pretty much self-disciplined. I could see from experience how other people got in trouble and I didn't want to go down that path. I kept my nose clean. I did my job.

Personal development at school and in the military

The similarities—as you advanced in pay grade, you became, through association with your leading chief and your division officer, more involved in work completion. Usually your division officer was the guy that made the big influence. If we did our job, he did his job and "looked good." It just worked that way. Bob Yarbrough had a great influence on me, because he was my English teacher in the twelfth grade, and he was a disciplinarian and he told you the way it was. I remember he gave us four hundred words to learn, actually four hundred seldom-used words, as he put it, and you had to know all four hundred of them. I remember one in particular was "schism," s-c-h-i-s-m. I don't think I ever heard Bob use "auspicious occasion."

The Christchurch experience and military life

That's a tough one. I know that the education I got here helped me immensely. I think coming from the public schools in White Stone, I probably learned more in the four years here than I'd have learned in a lifetime. Each situation in the service is somewhat different because it is somewhat unique. You travel all over the world and are involved with all different nationalities, different cultures. I don't think we had any foreign students at that time, but in the service you have all different nationalities. That's a significant learning process. The service promoted my work ethic. I am more goals-oriented. I want to see things happen. In that respect, in the service we were normally given a certain time frame to complete a certain specific task and I think that carried over when I retired. I basically worked at several different golf courses, started out at the bottom and ended up as the assistant maintenance director for Orange Park Country Club. The service set me for the proper context for achievement.

On the observation by Vice Admiral John W. Craine, Jr., '64, USN (Ret.), that at Christchurch and in the armed forces you are judged not "by who you are but by what you are"

Absolutely, and [I feel] exactly the same way. When I was on active duty, there were 597,000 people on active duty. There were less than 6,000 master chiefs [E-9 chief petty officers]. That's the top one percent. I thought I had accomplished a great deal until you and I talked about Admiral Craine. As a vice admiral he must be in the top 10,000[th] of a percent! Having come from Christchurch I thought I had hit a home run, but I wasn't even in the ballpark! There is also a drawback. Yes, you are judged by what you do, but it's a two-edged sword. The more you accomplish, guess who gets more responsibility, and sometimes that gets old. I went out and did this and this and this, and now you stick me with a job that no one else can complete, and you expect me to do it. You're sort of getting punished in that more is being asked of you, but that comes with the territory and if you accept it and go about and complete your task. I've got four Navy Achievement Medals and a Navy Commendation Medal for doing what I thought was right. I won a Golden Anchor and Silver Anchor for retention. I compare basically both the four years I spent at Christchurch and the thirty years I spent in the Navy as learning experiences that I am truly thankful that I had the opportunity to perform. My motto has always been, "Take nothing for granted," and that's how I operate.

LIEUTENANT COMMANDER ROGER A. GARLOW '57
U.S. Coast Guard (Cold War/Vietnam era/Iran-Iraq War)

Roger Garlow came to Christchurch School from Alexandria, Virginia, where he had attended St. Stephens School. He served as captain of the junior varsity football team and was active in the Social Affairs Committee at Christchurch. For many years, he attended alumni reunion weekend and rode his bicycle from his home in Newport News, Virginia. Roger enlisted in the United States Coast Guard in 1959 and served continuously until 1985. He began his Coast Guard career as an enlisted radioman, serving in ashore radio stations in such places as Bermuda and San Francisco. Following shore duty, he served in CGC *Taney* (WHEC-37), which was present at Pearl Harbor on December 7, 1941, and was the first warship underway. Subsequently, he served in CGC *Dexter* (WAVP-385), a former U.S. Navy seaplane tender, and during this tour of duty, he was selected for officer candidate school at Yorktown, from which he was graduated and commissioned an ensign. He later served in CGC *Unimak* (WHEC-379) and entered the maritime safety field of the service, which includes port safety, marine inspection and cleanup of hazardous materials and oil spills. In one tour of duty, he taught these subjects at the Coast Guard Training Center, Yorktown, Virginia. While assigned ashore at Yorktown, he attained the distinction of being awarded the Army Commendation Medal. He served in the Middle East, providing instruction to United Arab Emirate governmental officials in the theory and practical aspects of cleanup of oil spills.

Coming to Christchurch

[I] wasn't doing real well at St. Stephen's School in Alexandria, Virginia. I knew I needed a different environment. My parents had divorced, and staying at home was not the answer. I needed the structure that Christchurch could provide me. I was already two years behind things and didn't want to continue on that road. I did want to go to college and the only way I could was to clean up my act and do something about it. Thankfully, my dad paid my way through

Christchurch and I was able to get my grades up and graduate with a diploma. [I] was not sure about graduating with my class, but that is another story.

Significant influences at school

All the teachers were an influence in one way or another, most to the good and a couple not so good. They all contributed to my development and what I eventually became. Even the bad teachers contributed in that I had to make some decisions based on the way they handled some things. The decisions taught me how to stand up for my rights even under possible repercussions, and this learning I used many times in the military, not only for myself but also for the troops who at times had no one to stand up for them.

Choosing the armed forces

I joined the Coast Guard in June 1959, two years after I graduated from Christchurch. Due to financial constraints, I was not able to go to college full time. I did go to the University of Virginia night school in Arlington, which eventually became George Mason University. After two years of floating around, I realized I needed something to do. Vietnam was beginning to rear up and the draft was hot on my heels. With this in mind, I decided to go to St. Stephen's School and talk with one of my old teachers, Mr. Willie Wills, who also taught at Christchurch. We had a long talk and found out he'd been in the Coast Guard in World War II and had been a reserve officer. He suggested that the Coast Guard would be a good way to go since I was really not too sure as to where I was headed. By doing so, I could, after four years, go to college under the GI Bill. Well, twenty-six years later, I had still not gone to college, but I retired as a lieutenant commander. I started out enlisted, went to OCS [officer candidate school]. I can tell you that the education I got at Christchurch allowed me to pass all the tests for acceptance to OCS.

Service history in the military

I had several duty assignments. I started out enlisted and served as a Radioman [RM] at radio stations and two cutters. My first assignment was in the secondary radio station (call sign NOC) at the Coast Guard air detachment, Naval Air Station Bermuda . . . , where we provided search-and-rescue [SAR] operations in the Atlantic Ocean. Yes, this is the dreaded Bermuda Triangle. I was stationed there for three years . . . I was involved in many SAR cases. One that sticks out in my mind was one where we had to coordinate the meeting up of a U.S. Navy blimp that had been blown east of Bermuda by a very bad storm. We were, with the Navy, able to locate a destroyer and eventually get them together. The blimp dropped a line to the destroyer, and it was towed to Bermuda.

My next assignment was CGC *Taney* [WHEC-37], which was the first warship to get underway after the bombing of Pearl Harbor by the Japanese on December 7, 1941. We did SAR duties and Ocean Station duty[86] between Hawaii and San Francisco. The next sea duty I had was on CGC *Dexter* [WAVP-385] and from there I went to OCS. I was afraid my OCS stay was going to be very short . . . One of the things instructors did was give out demerits. The first day they gave out demerits, I managed to get ninety . . . If you got one hundred total during the course of the school you were kicked out. Somehow I managed to only get a couple more, and I survived to graduate as an ensign. I served on two cutters and then got into the marine safety aspect of the Coast Guard. It included port safety, marine inspection, cleanup of hazardous material and oil spills, and other duties. I taught the above for four years at the U.S. Coast Guard Training Center in Yorktown, Virginia. My last two years was as Coast Guard liaison to the U.S. Army Corps of Engineers. One trip was the United Arab Emirates [UAE] during the Iran-Iraq War to teach UAE officials how to clean up oil spills and also did this for United Nations training to Caribbean nations.

Communal living at Christchurch and in the military

Well, the experience of communal living was not new for me, since I had gone to Hargrave Military Academy when I was nine years old. I guess that enabled me to accept the dorm kind of living we had at Christchurch. The combination of the two enabled me to accept the military type of living without any problems. [I'd] been showering with guys all my life, I guess. However, the discipline aspect of both schools really helped, especially at boot camp, as I already knew most of the marching, drilling stuff. I had also handled guns from an early age and had been around water all my life.

Personal development at school and in the military

Overall, the one person who stood out and helped develop the way I would address myself to life and make decisions was Bob Yarbrough. Others had an impression, but not the way Mr. Yarbrough did. He believed in me and helped guide me along and taught me how to make correct decisions. He was also quick to correct me or take me to task when I was going in the wrong direction. At times when I had a decision to make, I would think back to Mr. Yarbrough and wonder what he would recommend. He always supported me, but I paid dearly for the wrong decisions, and that was the type of support I always tried to do with the guys who worked with/for me in the service. I always told my guys I would support them right or wrong, but they would pay for the wrong decisions after it was all over. Thankfully, ninety-nine percent of the time they made the right ones.

The Christchurch experience and military life

I actually think that my experiences at Christchurch reinforced my time in the service. What I learned at Christchurch from responsibility, ethics, leadership—and of course the education—was what enabled me to join the Coast Guard as enlisted and retire as a lieutenant commander. My twenty-six years of service was a direct result of what Christchurch ingrained into my mind, heart and soul. I made a lot of bad and good decisions during those twenty-six years—but mostly good decisions resulted from my experience of living and life at Christchurch.

LIEUTENANT H. MURRELL McLEOD '58
U. S. Navy (Cold War/Vietnam era)

H. Murrell McLeod entered Christchurch in 1955, from Richmond, Virginia, and established himself as a student leader. He earned the Bishop's Award, the highest honor Christchurch can bestow, as his son Weymouth Livingston McLeod '89 did thirty-one years later. Following graduation, he matriculated at Randolph-Macon College, where he earned his B.A. degree. He entered the Navy through officer candidate school and served on USS *Hancock* (CV-19) as R Division officer and assistant navigator in Vietnamese waters and on USS *Steinaker* (DD-863) as Damage Control Assistant and navigator in the Atlantic and Mediterranean.

Coming to Christchurch

My family dissolved, and my mother realized she couldn't handle me on her own. She indentured me to Christchurch. My brother, who was the child of her first marriage (she remarried my father) was given the opportunity to go to Christchurch. He is ten years older than I am. It was the logical thing to do, to consider Christchurch when she and my father separated.

Significant influences at school

This is not simple. Clearly Branch Spalding, who was headmaster when I applied was [a significant influence]. One morning when I stumbled out of bed, my mother asked me if I wanted to go to Christchurch School, and I said "no." Later that day, I was standing in front of him. He looked at me in his stern way and said, "Boy, if I give you a chance to come to Christchurch School, will you work?" I looked him in the eye and lied and said, "Yes sir." Several weeks later, my father was given the task of delivering me to the school. It was a rainy, cold day, and he pulled into the driveway, took my suitcase out of the car, said "Good luck," and drove off. I did not know which door to go into. That was my beginning at Christchurch School. I was damaged goods. I did not have a stable family life. You could say it was a dysfunctional family. I never had a functional one. Branch Spalding took a chance, and Bob Yarbrough came on the scene very quickly. There were two "Yarbroughs." One spelled his name with an "a" and the other, E. R. M. Yerburgh, with an "e." The one who was so important in my life spelled it with an "a" and was referred to as "Mr. A." He became headmaster after the corporate demise of Branch Spalding. Bob has been an influence in my life until he died a few years ago. Bob taught me that I had to be accountable for what I was asked to do, and that was not present in my life at home. He taught me that excellence was what everyone should strive for, that it was not extraordinary. On a positive note, Jim Taylor taught English, and was affectionately known as "Jungle Jim," or just "Jungle." He became someone I returned to see whenever I returned. My first day at Christchurch—there were twelve of us in the class—he said "Jack, read." No one did anything because there was no one named Jack in the class. On the third time he said, "New boy, read." I said, "My name is not Jack." Until he died, some years later, we had a wonderful relationship. He called me "Jack," and said, "You can do a lot more than you think. You can do things without being a perfectionist."

I was influenced by the community itself. I came from an unstable home. You tiptoed through life for fear of my father, who, when he drank, was not a benevolent character. You would go to any length to avoid an eruption, which would occur for no apparent reason. I didn't realize it when I came to Christchurch, but I was looking for a family. I began to sink into the comfort of a home at Christchurch. We got up together, all of us, went to class together, and went to chapel. It was literally a home, and for many years in the Navy, when I was asked to give a "home of record," I gave "Christchurch School, Christchurch, Virginia."

The honor system had an extraordinary influence on me. I can recall cash turning up in lost and found. I was not just in a family. There were consequences to my actions. There was a chap named Errett Callahan, a body-builder who served as a monitor, a person with authority and responsibility. When the lights went out, he would perch on a radiator. He could leap from radiator to radiator. You couldn't hear him coming. I wired a lamp in someone else's cubicle. I turned the unsuspecting chap's light on. Errett was furious and demanded that he turn the light out. The chap had no idea about why his light kept coming on. Errett finally decided to trace the wire, and of course it led back to my cubicle. I don't know how many hours of rockpile I received. I loved the whole thing, but it taught me that my actions had consequences.

Choosing the armed forces

One would think that the water-oriented school would be a strong influence for the Navy. We had an aboveground swimming pool, deteriorating to the point where it was dangerous, and a fleet of sailboats—Hamptons— that were lucky to float. That really wasn't an influence. My mother had three brothers, one of whom went to the Naval Academy and retired in the wartime rank of commodore—Thomas Garland Murrell, USN. My father had been in the Navy and retired as a lieutenant commander. I never related to his service. He ended up in the South Pacific on Espiritu Santo. My uncle Garland was a seagoing sailor, commander of a destroyer squadron, and I admired him so. My decision to go into the Navy came from a combination of influences at Christchurch, layered on top of my admiration for the commodore.

Service history in the military

I went to officer candidate school in Newport, Rhode Island, a four-month course, and my nemesis was marine navigation, a necessary requirement for being a naval officer. I watched my grade point average drop from as high as it could be. In my fifteenth week, my grade point average went below 3.5, so I was given the opportunity to roll back and graduate, which I did.

I was assigned to the ship's company of USS *Hancock* [CV-19], a World War II carrier, which started life as a straight deck carrier and had a conversion to an angled deck ship and had a steam catapult with serial number one, the first ship of the line to have steam catapults. The second day I was on board I was interviewed by the executive officer, who asked what I wanted to do, and I said, "Pretty much anything but engineering," whereupon I was assigned as Repair Division officer in engineering. It was to fight battle damage but also to be the ship's plumbers and electricians.

We sailed from the Pacific Coast to the PACFLT [U.S. Pacific Fleet] for our first deployment. Several things were happening then, not the least of which was the unpleasantness known as Vietnam. William Colby had become the CIA [Central Intelligence Agency] chief of station in Saigon. He was a Jedburgh, a tough dude, and he brought this out of the service and was recruited by the CIA. We were assigned the nastiest, least desirable station and were doing things we weren't supposed to do. For example, we carried barrels of powder that had a yellow-orange stripe and it turned out to be a herbicide that, when combined with other chemicals, could be sprayed on foliage, and that would kill the foliage and eliminate cover for the migrating Vietcong. You talk about hazardous duty! I recall taking barrels of this stuff and helping my folks roll it off the side of the ship from sponsons, for some of the barrels had rotted. I was up to my elbows in it and was exposed to it in its liquid form. The government now believes it was the presumptive cause of the cancer I experienced in 2007. We didn't know what it was and treated it very casually. We had older aircraft and were, in the words of one chap, expendable. I [later] discovered there is a USS *Hancock* Association, and I attended a reunion in 2010. I found out there were folks who were aboard when I was and recalled these things. At a table of eight there were five cancer survivors, and that is not a normal distribution. I have since then filed with the Veterans Administration. Whether anything comes out of it I do not know. I am being told these things did not happen.

The chief engineer asked me if I wanted duty outside the engineering department and when I said I did, I was assigned to be an assistant to the assistant navigator. One Chief Tarver befriended me and became my "sea daddy." When we were refueling, rearming or replenishing, we'd have an oiler or reefer [refrigerator ship] on one side and a destroyer on the other. He'd say, "Come with me and let me show you the real Navy." He'd point to a destroyer and say, "There's the real Navy." I transferred to a destroyer on the East Coast and chased submarines. We had some significant, highly sensitive missions involving Cuba. We communicated with the outside world only once a day, in the morning with Commander-in-Chief, Atlantic Fleet [CINCLANTFLT]. Our call sign was "Tomboy" and the call sign for CINCLANTFLT, as you might imagine, was "Jehovah." That was CINCLANTFLT's way of determining that we were still afloat.

USS *Steinaker* [DD-863] was a World War II Gearing-class destroyer that had been put through the Fleet Rehabilitation and Modernization program know as F-R-A-M, where they scraped the superstructure off and put an aluminum housing back on and rockets and so forth on. The first time they fired the five-inch guns, they warped every watertight door above the main deck, so they lost watertight integrity. It was a good concept. We worked with other destroyers. At one point we were supposed to locate an American submarine that was going to fire an ICBM prototype so we were supposed to be ringing the area, and we discovered a Russian nuclear submarine. After four days we surfaced the submarine, which was pretty amazing.

We had a storm in the Atlantic. I was navigator and DCA [Damage Control Assistant] and had about three other divisions in the engineering department. We had a hurricane. I don't recall how far the bridge is above the water, but we had green water breaking over the bridge. The captain decided it was time to strike the flagstaff on the fantail, and he issued me an order to go aft and do it or send someone else. I lashed myself to a third-class petty officer, who probably weighed ninety pounds, soaking wet. He lashed himself to the five-inch gun mount and we worked our way aft. You couldn't hear anything with the wind howling. I got the flagstaff collapsed. I couldn't hear the wave coming or him yelling at me, and had it not been for the webbing between the lifeline and the house line on a destroyer, I'd have been over the side. I always thought we had a pretty good proximity to Captain Queeg on the *Steinaker* at the time.

Communal living at Christchurch and in the military

At home I had a private room, and when I went to Christchurch, there was no privacy. The cubicles, our bedrooms, had no doors, they had no walls. There was nothing more than a partition. You could get a group of three people when someone was in the shower and take every bit of their clothing out of their cubicle and hide it so that when the victim returned, trying to get ready for dinner in three minutes, they had nothing to put on. I learned a great deal about communal living at Christchurch that prepared me in some ways.

When I went on board the carrier, I was assigned to the junior officers' quarters, which was below the foc'sle [forecastle] and the flight deck. The catapults on board were steam driven and drove the piston down a track, and how do you stop the piston? It pierces a seal and hits a tank of water contiguous with JO quarters. I learned to sleep through it, thanks to living at Christchurch. I learned that what one person did had an effect on everyone else. While others were learning that in the Navy, I already knew it. Before I went to Christchurch, I had the experiences with my father and the tirades were seemingly without cause. And when I got to the point where there was true discipline, it was a relief, and I didn't mind being held accountable. I avoided it because I did what I was told to do. I learned that at Christchurch.

Personal development at school and in the military

There were elements at Christchurch that I wish could be introduced in the military. At Christchurch it wasn't a wartime community. It wasn't democratic, but it was more democratic than the military. In the service, you rotated from one assignment to another and didn't count on taking friends with you. On the destroyer, there was an executive officer who thought I had career potential. He watched out for me in ways that I didn't often see in the military. He protected my back. He recommended me for duty as an admiral's aide. I saw that in abundance at Christchurch. The commanding officer of USS *Hancock*, Captain Arthur J. Brassfield, didn't have a lot of individual conversations with me unless they were duty related. We had some that were personal and he was supportive of my efforts and wanted me to make a career of the Navy and helped engineer my transfer to a destroyer.

The Christchurch experience and military life

The school taught me the basics of life—how to be honest and accountable, to see possibilities, to see that "can do" is the right way to think. The motto of *Hancock* was "Can do, Can do now." Having a fundamental concept of honesty, integrity, the work ethic and a sense of accountability will stand anyone in good stead in any walk of life. It made me enough of a standout on the carrier that the captain was helping me with my career, and enough of a standout on the destroyer that the executive officer was trying to get me to be an admiral's aide, which I saw as a positive thing. Unquestionably, Christchurch has influenced me every day that I have lived. In the military, I learned that friendships die, and it took me some time to overcome that. To its credit, being an officer in the Navy is a powerful legacy—not as powerful as being born in Virginia—but of the same ilk. I wouldn't trade it for anything.

On the observation by Vice Admiral John W. Craine, Jr., '64, USN (Ret.), that at Christchurch and in the armed forces you are judged not "by who you are but what you are"

It is quite true. You could talk a great game, like my boss the assistant navigator, whose job I took when his performance didn't match his talk. It is an extraordinary way of life. You don't get ahead by your heritage but by what you do—your performance. I never saw that before Bob Yarbrough took over as headmaster at Christchurch. Bob lived that. He was who he said he was. What you saw you got. That was Bob Yarbrough's life. He was not one face to students and another to everyone else. I think that Christchurch's core value was integrity, as is the Navy's.

HEALTH SERVICES TECHNICIAN
SECOND CLASS THOMAS G. MCMILLAN '59
U.S. Coast Guard (Cold War/ Vietnam era)

Tom McMillan, brother of Bob McMillan '61, "from the hills of West Virginia," was a strong citizen and performer at Christchurch. He was an outstanding student leader, evidenced by his service as president of the junior class, member of the student council and honor council and vice president of the senior class. He was, moreover, a member of the varsity track team and member of the varsity club. He enrolled in Randolph-Macon College and graduated from Morris Harvey College. He enlisted in the United States Coast Guard and attended Naval Hospital Corps School at the U.S. Naval Service Training Command, Great Lakes, near Chicago, Illinois, and upon successful completion, was assigned to shore duty with the Ninth Coast Guard District, commonly known as "The Guardians of the Great Lakes," in Cleveland, Ohio. (The titles are formal command designations.)

Coming to Christchurch

Our parents—Bob's and mine—felt that there was no question that the Charleston, West Virginia, public schools were not adequate in preparing us academically for further education. Therefore, they made the decision to send us to Christchurch School. They had done some research, and we had friends there. So it was an easy decision and it was such a beautiful environment. I think it was simply a great educational opportunity.

Significant influences at school

I'd say it was the professors, the teachers: Monte Miller, Bob Yarbrough, Hatcher Williams and "Spud" Parker. It was just a group of very good guys. I thought they were good teachers, but on top of that they were good guys. You had a lot of good participation. It was basically a fun environment to grow up in.

Choosing the armed forces

I went into the U.S. Coast Guard. At that time, the Vietnam War was getting pretty hot. I did not want to be drafted, but I did want to serve. I had some friends who had been in the Coast Guard and enjoyed it thoroughly, and therefore I joined. I had considered going to officer candidate school in the Navy and decided against it for no particular reason. The school and the waterfront really weren't that much of a factor. The water has always been in the forefront of my growing up and education. The Coast Guard is involved in water, and I can't completely say that that was the reason, but it makes sense.

Service history in the military

After boot camp at Cape May, New Jersey, I went to Great Lakes Naval Station for Naval Hospital Corps School. It was an absolutely outstanding school: There was intensive training, about a year-long program. It consisted of all areas of health care: nursing, nutrition, first aid and then combat-related medicine. As you know, the Hospital Corpsman, trained in the Navy or Coast Guard, is or can be part of the Fleet Marine Force. The sad part of this is that many of the really good guys in my company were killed in Vietnam. I had my orders to go to Coast Guard Activities Cleveland in the Ninth Coast Guard District. The guys who got their orders to go to the Marine Corps in Vietnam— and there were some very good guys—some were killed very soon after they got out there. You had a very good group of people with a very intensive training time. The Naval Station Great Lakes is one of the top training facilities for the entire U.S. Navy. It is very well done.

I went to Cleveland and I was on a buoy tender for a while, and then I went back to Charleston. I was a "six by six wonder." It was six months of basic training followed by six months of specialized training. I was very fortunate to be a hospital corpsman. I saw a lot of the Midwest. There was about a year of training, so I extended my six months of training. I then had service in the Coast Guard Reserve. I went to Yorktown, Virginia, Cape May, New Jersey and Galveston, Texas. I can't say that it was anything spectacular, but it was a lot of fun, education and meeting some great people.

Communal living at Christchurch and in the military

Any time you have a situation of the kind we had at Christchurch, you learn to adapt, you learn to do certain things you would not do if you were not in that environment, so it was a big help. Some of the people who showed up for boot camp had not had that experience and it was very difficult for them. As you know, boot camp is no fun. Everyone should do it, but it was not something I'd recommend. There's no question but that the Christchurch experience was helpful.

You had a different class of people at Christchurch, but there was not that big a difference in how you reacted and served in boot camp. You had the discipline as you had had it at school, but there was more discipline and strenuous jobs. It is a more serious situation in the military for you are training both for combat duty and the particular vocation you are in. At Christchurch School, by contrast, it was purely an educational experience, but you had the discipline, so along those lines they were similar, and school was a big help. The kids coming into the service who had not had that experience had a difficult time adjusting. It was little things like sleeping and taking showers with a bunch of guys and using communal heads.

Personal development at school and in the military

Basically, the faculty/staff were good people. Bob Yarbrough was really the standout, and even Bob Goodman, who was dean, was a good guy; and even "The Rev" [Charles V. Covell, Chaplain and Rector of Christ Episcopal Church] was all right. Monte Miller could seem distant and arrogant but was supportive and would listen to you. So was "Jungle" [James C. Taylor, Jr., Senior English Master]. It always seemed to me that Branch Spalding[87] wasn't as supportive, but he was on his way out. These men, and I almost forgot Ed Cox, were just good men who had a deep impact on us, in large part because of their devotion to the job of preparing boys for the transition to young adulthood.

In Coast Guard boot camp I had a DI [drill instructor] named Stryker. He was immaculate, with glistening shoes and the same sort of immediate impact on all of us who were there in a difficult, but ultimately rewarding time in our lives.

The Christchurch experience and military life

The service experience was a bit different because, as I have said, the people could be pretty different in basic ways, but we all had a way of coming together and accomplishing what was set before us to do, regardless of individual differences. Going back to an earlier question and my answer, serving in the armed forces—and this is, in my opinion, important—was something expected of those who had the benefits of a place like Christchurch. The only exception was for folks who had some physical disability. People like Mr. Yarbrough, who had served in the Army, "Jungle," who was a Navy man and Bob Goodman, who had been in the Army, were pretty clear on that point. It was a part of growing up, coming to adulthood.

On the observation by Vice Admiral John W. Craine, Jr., '64, USN (Ret.), that at Christchurch and in the armed forces, one is judged, not "by who you are but by what you are"

John is surely correct. There was always some sort of evaluation, where you were judged against your peers, and class standings were posted on a bulletin board outside the dean's office. It was a small school, and it didn't take long to discover what sort of person you were. This was particularly true in athletics. Really, this is what later life is all about, so I think we got good preparation for it at an early age.

Corporal F. Davis "Dave" Drumheller '60
U.S. Marine Corps (Cold War era)

Dave Drumheller entered Christchurch from Charleston, West Virginia, and graduated in June 1960. While at school, he amassed a splendid career as an athlete and, moreover, was a figure in student government. He earned the Christchurch Varsity C and was an officer in the following organizations: he served in the United States Marine Corps. He went through Recruit Training at Marine Corps Recruit Depot, Parris Island, South Carolina and at Camp Geiger and served in the Marine Corps Reserve in Company A of the 4th Combat Engineer Battalion, home-stationed at South Charleston, West Virginia.

Coming to Christchurch

I am not sure [how I came to be at Christchurch], though it may have been the fact that the public schools in Charleston, West Virginia, were integrated at the time. This was a feature that made the public schools undesirable for college preparation in the opinion of some citizens.

Significant influences at school

Grover Jones was a mentor and football coach. Gerry Cooper influenced my study of English literature, while Hatcher Williams was a strong scholar in the areas of grammar, spelling, punctuation and sentence structure. Bob Yarbrough's thorough grounding in vocabulary—with the Manter Hall School workbook—is something that I and others who took it remember with considerable fondness.

Choosing the armed forces

Christchurch did not have any influence on my joining the service. I flunked out of the University of Virginia following my freshman year and decided to join the U.S. Marine Corps. I did this without my parents' knowledge. It was one of the best experiences of my life. I guess I wanted to be the best of the best. The Marine Corps is and always has been the best of the best.

Service history in the military

I served in the Marine Corps Reserve program, which gave me boot camp and six months of active duty and five and a half years in the Marine Corps Reserve. I was in a combat engineering company and learned a lot about demolitions. In certain summer training periods we deployed to Vieques Island, a Navy amphibious training bombardment range on the eastern end of Puerto Rico.

Communal living at Christchurch and in the military

I suppose being on my own for four years in prep school prepared me for the Marine Corps. Being away from home was no big deal as it was for some. Athletic competition in prep school was helpful in getting me through boot camp and beyond.

Lieutenant (Junior Grade) Robert A. McMillan '61
U.S. Navy (Cold War/Vietnam era)

Bob McMillan '61 was a solid student, an athlete in basketball and a fine citizen of the school, evidenced by his service on the honor council and as a monitor. Following graduation in June 1961, he enrolled in and graduated from the University of North Carolina in 1965 as the Vietnam War was picking up tempo and United States involvement was increasing. Upon completion of officer candidate school (OCS) at Newport, Rhode Island, he was assigned to Beachmaster Unit Two, home-stationed at the Naval Amphibious Base, Little Creek, Virginia, and embarked aboard various amphibious ships. While embarked on board USS *Spiegel Grove* (LSD-32),[88] he qualified as an underway officer of the deck for task force operations. Released from active duty as a lieutenant (junior grade), he earned a master's degree in business administration at Emory University. He is president and owner of the Jefferson Distributing Company of Martinsburg, West Virginia.

Coming to Christchurch

[How I came to Christchurch is] a question I've thought about, and I'll be real frank: I was not applying myself at junior high school in Charleston, West Virginia—Horace Mann Junior High School. My father decided it was time for me to buckle down, and I had a brother at Christchurch, so it was pretty simple for me to enroll. I came to Christchurch thinking [that] after finishing the ninth grade I was going to be a tenth grader. When I got here, my proficiency in English was not quite what Mr. Yarbrough wanted, and they put me back. I fought that. I kept telling everybody I was a tenth grader and every time they would see me, I'd be in the ninth-grade English class. I did stay back and I even went to summer school thinking that would work and I'd get jumped ahead, but that didn't work, so I spent four years at Christchurch.

As I've reflected on that with my classmates here at our fiftieth reunion, it was the right decision for me. I was a babe in the woods, I had an attitude problem. I knew all the answers—my kids call me the answer man. Christchurch made me a believer that if you keep your mouth shut and listen, you'll have them. There were excellent masters at the time who dedicated themselves to teaching. I struggled through four years, which I still describe as the four most difficult years of my life.

Significant influences at school

My English skills were not good. I can remember Mr. Yarbrough's vocabulary class, where every word he gave us was a new word for me. I will always remember Mr. Yarbrough's diligence in teaching us vocabulary. Mr. Taylor was also an influence on me. I always enjoyed getting my papers with his wonderful penmanship and his red ink all over them. I played athletics, and Grover Jones, who was our basketball coach, did not like basketball. I learned to get along with Coach Jones, and I learned a lot from him. He was a never-give-up kind of guy. Now Mr. Davies—I played basketball and baseball—he was just a totally different kind of guy. I enjoyed him and I enjoyed them all. I could go down a list of masters who were here when I was, for they all left an impression on me.

Choosing the armed forces

Being from the hills of West Virginia, one of the greatest things about Christchurch was being able to look out and see that beautiful Rappahannock River and know that it was brackish, or salty. I can't say that I had seawater in my veins. When I graduated from the University of North Carolina in 1965, as we all know, the Vietnam War was heating up and I was in a position to go to graduate business school. I wrote the draft board, and they told me as long as I could get my MBA from June and be done by October 1965, I'd be okay, and I said, "That won't work." So I looked around for any opportunity available other than being drafted into the Army. The Navy officer candidate school [OCS] came up. It came up that a lot of my friends who graduated with me and were a lot smarter than me did NROTC [Naval ROTC]. If you graduated from college up to the end of 1966, you got your commission and only had a two-year obligation. I wasn't smart enough to do that . . . When I got ready for OCS, there was a wait-list, and I didn't get accepted until January 1966. That was probably the second most difficult time of my life, going through officer candidate school. When you have to be timed to do anything, it is difficult. Christchurch wasn't difficult, because you got an exam paper and you had time to do it. In OCS all quizzes were limited to about fifteen minutes . . . Through the Christchurch experience and knowing you just had to persevere, I made it through officer candidate school.

Service history in the military

Well, I got my commission and at that time you probably didn't get too much opportunity to voice your preference. You just walked in after you got your commission, and they gave you your assignment. I was assigned to the Naval Beach Group Beachmaster Unit Two, and I went to one of my instructors, who was a chief petty officer, and I said, "Chief, what are Beachmasters?" He said, "I know full well what they are because during World War II, on the invasion of Normandy, Beachmasters went in on the third wave, and they had a life expectancy of about thirty seconds." I thought that didn't sound very good. You didn't volunteer, you just got assigned to whatever command was deemed appropriate by detailers in the Bureau of Naval Personnel such as the Naval Beach Group. I had a wonderful experience there. I was stationed at Little Creek, Norfolk, Virginia.

You mentioned hazardous duty. At one point I was over in the Mediterranean, at the time of the Israeli and Egyptian six- or seven-day war, and the Greeks and the Turks were quarreling. There was something going on Cyprus. All of it was very non-hazardous, I might add. Then I was assigned to go to Vietnam, and I went to counterinsurgency school in Panama and— you'll laugh at this—I was a senior LTJG [lieutenant junior grade].[89] We had another LTJG who was supposed to report to the ship in San Diego. I was called back because the guy on assignment in the Caribbean had some problem. I've forgotten what it was. He was an airdale (naval aviator) who had gotten washed out for a hearing problem. I was sent to the Caribbean and never did go to Vietnam, much to my disappointment. I did finish my three and a half years in the Naval Beach Group in Beachmaster Unit Two, and it was very rewarding.

My Christchurch experiences taught me to respect my shipmates . . . As you remember, in the period '57 to '61 at Christchurch you were limited in the amount of space you had, i.e., a cubicle where you lived. I was placed on board a number of ships as a Beachmaster. I was an officer and had a stateroom, which was plush compared to Christchurch! I was an embarked troop as part of the Battalion Landing Team, but the XO [executive officer] of every ship in which I was embarked said, "LTJG McMillan, you will stand watch," even though I was not in the ship's company. At one point, I was qualified as an officer of the deck underway for formation steaming[90] by Captain D. A. York, who was a destroyer guy. I guess he was striking for admiral, for he had been given command of a flat-bottomed amphibious ship, USS *Spiegel Grove* (LSD-32).[91]

Communal living at Christchurch and in the military

If I had not had the Christchurch experience . . .

As you well know, going into the lavatory at Christchurch school—(laughter)—was an experience all in itself. [There were] the communal showers and toilets without stalls. You get the drift. You recall the tight quarters. The troops I was assigned to supervise in the Beachmaster detachment were embarked troops on different amphibious ships. They had a tougher time than I did because I had an individual stateroom. Every time we deployed, we'd go in with marines and land on various beaches in the Med and Europe and sometimes in Central and South America. You had to learn to adjust to a lot of different situations but it was always with your troops.

We tried to be a little bit individualistic at Christchurch, but you soon learned that you were part of a bigger unit—your class, your dorm. You had to learn to share space with other people . . . I saw a sign here, "Respect your fellow classmate." Christchurch did a lot. I had a wonderful Navy experience without any difficulty. I always accuse my wife—She'd have spent half of her time in the brig, for she doesn't learn to follow my orders. (laughter)

I'll say that the four most difficult years of my life were Christchurch School: adjusting to when you're told to do something, doing it. When I went to officer candidate school, I fell right in line and remembered my experiences at Christchurch School.

You have to remember that I had a four-year sabbatical as a "social animal" at the University of North Carolina, where I got a great social education. I am not sure whether I met the educational requirements. Christchurch was a discipline that I learned to respect and I am sure I had a few hours of rockpile, but I never faced a court martial or spent any time in the brig.

Personal development at school and in the military

I had wonderful times here and needed to be mentored by people like Mr. Yarbrough, Mr. Parker or Gerry Cooper. I even respected Grover Jones, who had a pretty sharp edge on him. So when I got in the service, I was going to officer candidate school and just wanted to survive. I had a Navy captain who ran the Beach Group who was a SEAL and at the time the SEALS were just beginning. For fun he used to like to swim into Haiphong Harbor and mine the nets to keep the submarines from coming out. He did seven tours in Vietnam. And I respected Captain Knight. He was a real mentor to me and gave me a real long, hard talk about making the Navy a career. I saw that with Captain Knight and Captain York on the USS *Spiegel Grove*, who had to work hard with me to get me qualified as an underway officer of the deck for formation steaming.

If I hadn't had that kind of relationship, I might not have the same positive feeling toward the Navy. Captain York, when we were underway, would invite me to his cabin to have lunch. I was probably one of the few officers he ever did that with. That type of experience I'd reflect on, as I did the associations with Christchurch masters.

The Christchurch experience and the military

I think they were hand in hand. You know the discipline I learned at Christchurch helped. I don't think I'd have ever made it out of a public high school. I knew I had to buckle down and study hard and people encouraged me to do it. In the service, there was a degree of leaning back on my tenacity I'd had to show in my four years at Christchurch that helped me. You know, I enjoyed the service. I was at sea for sixty-one days one time, and that can be a challenge. I am sure there were experiences I learned in the Navy that I never had at Christchurch and vice versa, but the two of them together made me a much, much better person.

When I was in the active duty Navy I always intended to be a reserve officer. I always had a fear that I would revert back to my college days, but after four years in the Navy and reflecting on the seriousness of what I was doing there I went to graduate business school. I was married and had a child on the way, and I buckled down and did what had to be done. That was what the service was. You were given orders and you didn't dispute the orders. I felt that way about going to business school. You did what you were told to do and you expected that of those you gave orders to. I had a different career in the first eight or nine years out of graduate school. I was in the real estate business with Mobil Oil; and I had an insurance business before I was fortunate enough to buy my own business. There is a discipline in that for, as we all know, running a business has its moments.

On the observation by Vice Admiral John W. Craine, Jr., '64, USN (Ret.), that at Christchurch and in the armed forces, you are judged not "by who you are but by what you are"

John and I became re-acquainted when we served on the board of Christchurch School a number of years ago, and I respect John tremendously. Anyone who rises to the rank of admiral is a hero and has done wonderful things in the service. I think that what he has said is true. I think we can all go in and say I am a graduate of the University of North Carolina or the University of Virginia and that makes you something. You have to perform in order to be recognized in a positive manner. You can't stand up and say you're an admiral and not perform as an admiral. I respect that, and I think that's a true statement. I think as we go through life we have our moments when we think we're pretty much the most important thing. We walk on the beach, as I tell my wife, and we watch the waves wash the sand up and I think of our lives: we're here for a short period of time, and you make out of it what you can. The Navy surely helped me tremendously.

Vice Admiral John W. Craine, Jr., '64
U.S. Navy (Cold War era/Vietnam War/ Humanitarian Assistance/War on Terror)

John Craine entered Christchurch as a day student from Urbanna, a town he described in the 1964 *Tides* as "a Garden of Eden," and was a strong contributor to the community. He particularly excelled in soccer and was a monitor during the last of his five years at Christchurch. He was, moreover, a solid student. Following his June 1964 graduation, he enrolled in and was graduated from Randolph-Macon College in Ashland, Virginia. Subsequently, he was selected for U.S. Navy flight training as an aviation officer candidate and earned his wings in November 1968. He served in various fleet aviation squadrons, taking on progressively more responsibility in increasingly difficult jobs, such as that of squadron maintenance officer. He is a distinguished graduate of the Air War College at Maxwell Air Force Base, Alabama. He was commanding officer of Fighter Squadron Eighty-Four and Naval Air Station Oceana, Virginia; served as air operations officer for Cruiser Destroyer Group Eight[92] in Norfolk, Virginia; and was special assistant for Flag Matters in the Bureau of Naval Personnel. He was commanding officer of the Naval Air Station at Oceana, Virginia, and was then promoted to flag rank. He served as Commander Shore Activities Atlantic Fleet and in that job was responsible for supervision of humanitarian care efforts given to Haitian migrants, and later Cubans,[93] who fled their homeland and were housed at the Naval Base, Guantanamo Bay, Cuba. He served in the Program Appraisal Division in the Office of the Chief of Naval Operations in the Pentagon and finally as Chief of Naval Education and Training at Naval Air Station, Pensacola, Florida.

Coming to Christchurch

Living in Urbanna, less than a mile and a half from Christchurch, made it an easy choice. My parents wanted to make sure I had the best education available. They knew the headmaster, Branch Spalding, when I applied, and Bob Yarbrough, who was headmaster the five years I was there. I went to summer school before I entered the ninth grade. I needed to brush up on [my] English skills and grammar, and Christchurch certainly helped me do that. It took me five years to graduate but it was a wonderful experience.

Significant influences at school

Other than my mother, my father and my wife, Wendy, my teachers at Christchurch had more influence on me than anyone else has in my life. I still fall back on the experiences at Christchurch and the interactions with teachers there.

The teacher who had the greatest influence on my life was Mr. Bill Davies. He was a teacher at the school the entire time I was there. Not only was he the athletic director and baseball coach, but he was also the biology teacher, and I can remember in biology class having to draw and label various diagrams of frog legs and eels as we dissected them. The drawings had to be very precise. He was trying to instill the discipline and work ethic [we would need] to be successful in life. One event I can remember as if it were yesterday was being on the athletic field with him before baseball practice. He had received a letter from a friend who was a test pilot at Patuxent River Naval Air Station, testing the experimental aircraft POGO, designated the Convair XFY1 and Lockheed XFV1, a vertical takeoff and landing aircraft which had huge counter-rotating propellers. In this letter, which he read to me, he was telling Mr. Davies what it was like on takeoff. He described the acceleration forces as being so great that when he looked into the cockpit mirrors during takeoff, he could see that the "G" forces [acceleration] had pulled his facial flesh down around his chin and neck. I thought at the time, that's what I want to do one day—be a pilot.

There was another gentleman, Colonel Nunn, who was a history teacher and retired Army officer. He was also the track coach and soccer coach—and he, too, demanded an awful lot of us in the classroom and on the athletic field. I can remember going into his office, which was also the history classroom, complaining about a grade, and I didn't get very far. The next thing I knew he was ushering me out the door while saying, "Learn the material, and the grades will come automatically." While the words did not mean much to me then as they did later in life, I applied that principle throughout my military career. Work hard and good things will happen. It is people like Mr. Davies, and Colonel Nunn, Mr. Williams, Mr. Taylor and Mr. Yarbrough, and others who taught and mentored me during that five-year period, that had such a positive impact on my life.

Choosing the armed forces

I can remember when I was about six years old, sitting on my grandfather's knee, asking what I was going to do when I grew up. He said I'd finish elementary school, then go off to high school and college and then enter the armed forces. I never forgot that, and when I was in my sophomore year at Christchurch, I realized I had only two years before college and needed to think about the armed forces military academies of ROTC programs.

I ended up at Randolph-Macon College, which didn't have an ROTC program, but keeping my dream to fly alive, I earned my private pilot's license while I was there. That gave me a leg up in applying to the Navy and being selected to fly jets. I talked to my father, who had been in the Navy, and my grandfather, who had also been in the Army, and my future father-in-law, who was an Air Force general. I remember my dad saying that if you're in the Army, you'll be outdoors a lot, and you won't have hot and cold running water, and in the Navy you'll have that, and you'll get three square meals a day. I didn't know what a square meal was, and I learned that on Navy ships, meals are served on square aluminum trays. But it was really that afternoon out on that athletic field with Mr. Davies that solidified my desire to be a pilot, and I could do that in the Navy, the Marine Corps or the Air Force.

Later that spring when I was driving around Virginia Beach with my girlfriend, who was a student at St. Margaret's School, we just happened to drive by Naval Air Station Oceana and there was an F-8 Crusader at the end of the runway with its engines running up. When it went into afterburner, all I could remember was hearing an explosion and seeing a big ball of fire come roaring out of the back of that jet, and in a flash it was down the runway and gone. My eyes must have been as big as saucers, and I said to my girlfriend that that was what I wanted to do someday: fly a plane. Well, not only did that dream of flying Navy fighters come true, but that girlfriend became my wife, and I ended up commanding that air station many years later.

Service history in the military

I was a naval aviator—fighter pilot—and I spent most of my time flying from various aircraft carriers in the F-4 Phantom and later the F-14 Tomcat. I was initially assigned to a fighter squadron embarked on USS *Saratoga* [CV-60]. We made an initial deployment to the Mediterranean. When we were back for just a few months, we were told that we would deploy again. It was an emergency deployment, with four days notice. We learned after we were at sea and the last mail call that we were going to Vietnam. What had started out as a four-month deployment because the ship was going into the yard for an overhaul turned out to be a year-long stint off North and South Vietnam.

I flew 114 combat missions. Some were a bit more interesting than others and more challenging, because we were doing Alpha strikes. These were big missions, sometimes involving more than one carrier, lots of aircraft going in conducting coordinated strikes in North Vietnam. We ended up getting a lot of surface-to-air missiles [SAMs] and Triple A [anti-aircraft artillery] fired at us. I was very fortunate that I never had to eject out of an airplane, but I had squadron mates who did. It was an interesting year, to say the least!

Following that squadron tour, each assignment seemed to be better than the one before, in terms of opportunity, responsibility and challenge. My tour as a tactical fighter instructor at Key West, an idyllic place to raise a family, living on the water with a boat in our back yard, flying two or three flights a day, teaching fighter tactics to pilots, made for a tremendously rewarding experience. It doesn't get much better than that!

Being selected to be commanding officer of a squadron was a tremendous honor and along with it came the accountability for leading those men on deployments. The assignment in which I thought I was able to make the biggest difference was my last—Chief of Naval Education and Training. I knew that I was going to have the opportunity to impact peoples' lives. For example, when I was in the position, we created a program known as the "Navy College," which provided service members the opportunity to get a college degree while they were on active duty, something Chief of Naval Operations Admiral Jay Johnson wanted. The program has made a big difference in the lives of our sailors, something I didn't fully appreciate until I was out of the Navy and president of SUNY Maritime College, where we had a Naval Reserve Officers Training Corps Unit [NROTC] and Seaman to Admiral-21 students, as we called the students selected for the Navy College Program. Seeing them fully participate in the college programs, including varsity sports, and having them tell me how much they appreciated the opportunity this program provided them was tremendously rewarding. While I was at the college, eight out of nine valedictorians were Navy or Marine Corps students. We were able to change other programs that enhanced sailors' abilities to go off and do things they had never had the opportunity to do before. To me that was a very rewarding time.

Communal living at Christchurch and in the military

I was a day student, so my community experience was a bit different from most students at Christchurch. I had the best of two worlds. I got to sleep at home, and after breakfast with my family I went off to school, which was like a country club experience. Yes, there were rigorous academics in the morning, but the afternoons were filled with athletics. It was the teachers who made the Christchurch experience such a positive, life-changing and enhancing experience . . . They were teacher/coaches—they did double duty and in some cases triple duty. They expected a lot from us both in the classroom and on the athletic field, and there was a good dose of discipline and decorum in between. We dressed in coat and tie for dinner. As I look back on it, they were preparing us for the rest of our lives. The discipline, manners and moral values and the work ethic they instilled, in the classroom and on the athletic field, were ingrained in each of us.

In soccer, for example, Colonel Nunn was an exacting, tough disciplinarian. I can remember his pulling us off the field and sitting us down in a classroom and chewing us out for not giving it our all. He didn't expect 100%; he expected 110% every day and every minute, on the field as well as in the classroom. I can recall a term paper where he took off twenty-five points for neatness. My mother had offered to type the paper, and I said, "No, I am going to print this and make it easier for him to read." I had strikeovers and corrections with my pen that he didn't appreciate, and he was absolutely right. Living at home but spending about eighty percent of the day at school, of course, you got to know everybody. You learned how to function as a group, or a team. That experience has stayed with me throughout my life.

I can't say enough about how Christchurch prepared me for what I encountered in the rest of my life, from raising a family to serving in the armed forces. It also provided me the opportunity to meet the love of my life, who was a student at St. Margaret's. Needless to say, I am eternally grateful for the opportunity and experience.

Personal development at school and in the military

As I have mentioned, we were always expected to be prepared. As you know, there was a dress code at the time. It wasn't just how well you did your schoolwork and whether you got your homework done—it was how well you comported yourself, in the classroom, on the athletic field and around campus. You "wore the cloth of the school," so to speak, and you wore a coat and tie. I can remember it as if it were yesterday: the headmaster, Mr. Yarbrough[94], who was also known as "Bob A." or "The Hawk," teaching us that at church you wore a conservative tie, white shirt and a dark suit, and I still wear that "uniform" when I go to church.

I thank Bob Yarbrough to this day and can cite examples like that some fifty years later and the influence they have on my life. They were the people you respected, admired and looked up to. You wanted to do your best by them and make them proud, whether in class or on the playing field. It is the same being an officer and doing your best for your division officer, department head or commanding officer. Because of Christchurch mentors and teachers, what was expected in the military was a seamless transition.

The Christchurch experience and military life

The people about whom I have spoken—those at Christchurch who had a strong influence in my life—had all served in the armed forces. Mr. Davies was in the Army Air Corps; Colonel Nunn in the Army; Captain Riley a Navy submariner; Commander Smart a Navy chaplain; Mr. Taylor, who had served in the Navy. All of them brought with them to the school some of what they had learned during their time serving their country. When you are dealing with peoples' lives, you can't do it with a cavalier attitude, and there was nothing cavalier that I can remember about Christchurch. As I served in my squadrons, there were people from all different walks of life, some from different socioeconomic backgrounds, and it really didn't matter. Everyone came together and worked hard to make sure that whatever mission was at hand, it was done the right way. When I dealt with some pretty difficult things, like having to inform a sailor of a death in his or her family or tell the parents of the death of their son or daughter, I thought back to my days at Christchurch and what I had learned there.

You once observed that in the Navy, as it was at Christchurch, you are judged not by who you are but what you are. Do you have any further thoughts on this?

Talk is cheap. It is those who take action, do the tasks, take the risks, who make the difference. And when it all comes down to it, it doesn't matter where you come from, who you are, what your background is—what is important is what you actually do. I have studied and talked a lot about leadership over the years. Effective leadership boils down to several things. As a leader, you have to trust yourself, your gut instincts, and you must trust those with whom you work. You must empower those with whom you work to do their job. I can recall General Kelley [Paul X., USMC] talking about the power of empowerment. You explain what you want done but not how to do it. Let those who are actually doing the task do it, and get the personal satisfaction out of doing it, rather than telling them step by step how to do it.

This is something we all learned at Christchurch. Our teachers gave us assignments, but it was up to us to figure out how to accomplish it. In the end, it is those who actually get in the arena, who "roll up their sleeves" and complete the task at hand, who make the difference. It is they who make a difference in peoples' lives by taking on tough jobs that no one wants, and who are not satisfied with the status quo and want to make things better for their people. One can look good, speak eloquently about what needs to be done, but it is all for naught unless one actually gets involved and accomplishes what needs to be done. What really matters is doing the job and doing it better than expected. For me, it is what made my time at Christchurch so valuable, for we were always expected to exceed expectations. I can say without reservation that I would not be where I am today and would not have achieved or been as successful as I am had it not been for those five years I spent at Christchurch School. I will forever be grateful for the school and its fine teachers, who made such a positive difference in my life.

Sergeant Joseph B. Farrar '65
U. S. Army (Special Forces) (Cold War era/Vietnam War)

Joe Farrar, who entered the school from Blackstone, Virginia, was an accomplished athlete and a competent scholar and, above all, a friend to others. He is best remembered for his kindness to others, whether they were older or younger. He earned the Varsity C in football, soccer and track and was a monitor on the long end of the third floor of Bishop Brown, a venue populated by spirited residents who needed strong supervision and guidance. He enrolled in the Virginia Military Institute and, following service as a medic in the Army in Vietnam assigned to the Special Operations Group (SOG[95]), graduated from The University of the South, atop the mountain in Sewanee, Tennessee. He was for many years a highly successful securities broker in Charlottesville, Virginia and served in the Development Office of Christchurch School.

Coming to Christchurch

I was fortunate. I had concerned parents who saw that their eldest child was a very mediocre student, having deficiencies in algebra 2 and plane geometry. My father was down in Tidewater, Virginia, on business and went by Christchurch School to investigate summer school opportunities. I think "Jungle" Jim Taylor gave him a tour of the school. Jim Taylor was a World War II veteran, as was my father [Distinguished Service Cross in the Battle of the Bulge] and was an excellent salesman for the school. I was enrolled in the summer school and the rest is history.

I had a good summer there. Bob Gillespie in plane geometry and Jim Taylor in algebra 2 were good instructors. The first two weeks I was there, I sat at "Jungle's" table . . . He wanted to check me out. I think he was impressed with my father—like father, like son. They found out I was of good moral character and had some leadership ability, and Archie Soucek found out I could play football. I was also with Jim Taylor and Herb Wyatt when the school had trouble with the "Guinea Men."[96] My father came down and Bob Yarbrough told him: we would like to have Joe attend Christchurch very much, but we won't take him for just one year. I had to drop back a year, but that was amenable to me. Course offerings were diverse enough, and I came from a small school. I never had to take anything over. That was a high point in my life. I wish I had applied myself more fully to academic life.

Significant influences at school

All the masters had an influence on me, each in his own way. However, the ones I best remember were Jim Taylor, Richard J. M. Poulson, Colonel William A. Nunn, Jr., [USA (Ret.)] and Commander [Chaplain Corps] John Smart [USN (Ret.)]. These men, all retired military, stand out above the rest. Two taught me and two coached me; all mentored me. Jim Taylor wanted me to come to Christchurch, for he felt the school could help me and that I could add something to the school. He pushed for me to have that opportunity, and he gave me a job with the rental athletic gear office that he ran at the school.

Colonel Nunn was my soccer and track coach. The Colonel had the respect of every boy on the campus. He was a big, imposing man who could silence a group of chattering boys with a booming "At ease!" The force of his character and personality led us to victory more than once. In particular was the day the "unlucky thirteen" big "drinking scandal" broke. Floyd Milby, the school maintenance superintendent, was out walking his dog one day behind the school and fell into "the hideout," stood up and fell in again, because it had two levels. The two ringleaders had kept a ledger of who drank what and when. Drinking alcoholic beverages was an expulsion offense at Christchurch.[97] When we loaded the bus that afternoon to go to Richmond to play Collegiate School, there were more boys getting off the bus than on. The Colonel, after his obligatory "At ease," said, "I have never lost to Grover Jones and I don't intend to start today." We won 2-0. He willed us to win that game. He lost half of his team as a result of the dismissals, and we had to bring players up from the junior varsity just to practice. He continued to exert his will, and we went on to win the state championship—we were 8-0-1. His force of character and leadership, getting us to play beyond our ability, led the team to an 8-0-1 season and being declared the high school soccer champions of Virginia. He was a man you didn't want to disappoint.

Richard Jasper Metcalfe Poulson, or "the Rock," as we called him behind his back, came into my life the summer of my senior year. He was my assistant football and track coach and I was his dormitory prefect. He had graduated from Randolph-Macon Academy and had a tour in the Army. He was an ex-rugby player and had a cute wife we called "Pebbles." Dick was another master you didn't want to disappoint. I ran anchorman on the mile relay team that still holds the school record. Dick told the Colonel that although I wasn't the fastest quarter-miler on the team, he knew my teammates would get me the baton with a lead, and he knew I would never relinquish it. He was right. We never were beaten in that year, 1965, in the mile relay. The Colonel and Rock talked the talk and walked the walk.

Choosing the armed forces

After graduating from Christchurch, I attended VMI [Virginia Military Institute] for a year. It was not what I considered a good year for me. I decided that if I were going to endure the military, I would like them to pay me instead of my parents and me paying for the opportunity to make me miserable. I joined the Army so I could jump from a perfectly good airplane.

Service history in the military

After completing basic and advanced Individual Infantry Training, I volunteered for Jump School [parachute training]. After completing Jump School, I was accepted for Special Forces Training. I spent about eighteen months training in North Carolina, Texas, Alabama and Panama. In October 1968 I was assigned as a Special Forces medic in Vietnam with the Military Assistance Advisory Command Vietnam [MACV], Studies and Operations Group. This was a top secret black operations group[98] that was awarded the Army's Presidential Unit Citation. The MACV-SOG reconnaissance teams, composed of Army Special Forces soldiers and indigenous personnel, penetrated the enemy's most dangerous redoubts in the Laotian jungle wilderness and sanctuaries of eastern Cambodia. Pursued by human trackers and even bloodhounds, these small teams out-maneuvered and outfought and outran the numerically superior foe to uncover enemy facilities, rescue downed pilots, plant wiretaps, mines and electronic sensors, capture valuable enemy prisoners, ambush convoys, assess potential targets for B-52 strikes and generally inflict casualties on the enemy, out of all proportion to their forces. When enemy countermeasures became dangerous and effective, SOG operators developed their own countermeasures, from high altitude parachuting an unusual explosive devices to tactics as old as the French and Indian War. Fighting alongside Montagnard, Chinese Mung, Cambodian and Vietnamese allies, Special Forces Hatchet Force companies stayed during the raids against key enemy facilities in Cambodia, overran major munitions and supply stockpiles and blocked enemy highways to choke off the flow of supplies to South Vietnam. During my tour in Southeast Asia, I supported and participated in Hatchet Forces reconnaissance and rescue and recovery missions known as Bright Light.

Communal living at Christchurch and in the military

I didn't really experience communal living at Christchurch. I had only one roommate or lived alone. My experience at VMI, where I had three roommates and folding cots, was my first experience with communal living. I never had problems with discipline at Christchurch. I was always busy with studies, homework and sports. I thought they filled up my time, and by the end of the day I was ready to get some rest.

Personal development at school and in the military

There was a great similarity between faculty personalities and military personalities. Both groups not only taught the walk, but they lived the walk. The time frame was more critical, because the men they were training might, and very many times were, the same men they would be leading and fighting with. You tend not to cut corners with people who may well have your back in a combat situation. Time in the service was more critical.

The Christchurch experience and military life

I think that probably the experiences I had in the service reinforce the experiences I had in school. In school, they tried to emphasize that a lot of this was teamwork and that you had to push yourself above mere individual achievement. You had to put the team above yourself.

On the observation by Vice Admiral John W. Craine, Jr., '64, USN (Ret.), that at Christchurch and in the armed forces you are judged not "by who you are but what you are"

I would agree with John that in the military, as at Christchurch, you are judged not by who you are but what you are. If you talk a good game, you had better be able to play a good game, and it was better not to talk at all and let your actions speak for you. In combat, you are put in a great crucible and subject to great pressure. How you react reveals a great deal to yourself, and others.

Captain F. Breckinridge Montague '66
U.S. Navy (Vietnam War/Cold War era)

Breck Montague was a leader and fine athlete at Christchurch, evidenced by earning the Varsity C in cross-country and two-mile track that he recalls as a way of building self-esteem. Following his June 1966 graduation, he enrolled in and was graduated from Hampden-Sydney College with a Bachelor of Arts degree in economics. He also holds master's degrees from George Washington University and the University of Rhode Island in public and international affairs and coastal zone management. In 1968, he enlisted in the Naval Reserve and, following Reserve Officer Candidate (ROC) training, was commissioned an ensign in October 1970. He served at sea for three years on USS *Sioux* (ATF-75), including four months conducting diving and salvage operations in Vietnamese waters, advancing to the post of executive officer. He was officer-in-charge of a crew on the *Sioux* who assisted sixty Turkish crewmen in sailing the ship to Turkey when she was sold to the Turkish government. Following release from active duty as a lieutenant (junior grade), he affiliated with the active Navy Reserve and served in various Mobile Diving and Salvage Units to include the billet of commanding officer. He was retired from the active Navy Reserve in 2000. Breck Montague is presently an assistant vice president with Merrill Lynch financial advisors in Williamsburg, Virginia, and has had a long and successful career in the financial services/investment banking field. Moreover, he is active in the affairs of his home community, Gloucester County, Virginia. He has, among other things, served as the senior warden of Ware Episcopal Church in Gloucester and as president of the Friends of Dragon Run Land Conservancy, as well as serving on the Board of Governors of Christchurch School and the Gloucester Community Foundation. He has served on the board of Preservation Virginia, formerly known as the APVA (Association for the Preservation of Virginia Antiquities).

Coming to Christchurch

My family lived in Urbanna nearby. There were two factors—I had just gotten accepted to Episcopal High School in Alexandria and had just finished summer school at Christchurch. Episcopal officials didn't think too much of that and wanted me to go back a grade, and I didn't want to do that, nor did my parents. I matriculated after skipping the eighth grade into the ninth grade at Christchurch.

Significant influences at school

It all goes by in a blur. My junior year it was English master Dick "Rock" Poulson. We called him "Rock" Poulson because he was tough as nails. I remember him because I grew to love English literature under him. He happened to be the track coach and I started running track. Dick Poulson was an influence just because he demanded academic excellence. The other was Captain [Frederic D.] Riley [USN (Ret.)],[99] who I probably had when I was a day student. Captain Riley was an incredibly decent, patient man who took a kid who "didn't get it the first time and made sure he got it the second time." I appreciated that.

Choosing the armed forces

Family tradition played a big part. My father was a career marine officer and retired as a brigadier general. I was one year behind Lewis Puller and General Puller was a family friend. There was another adult career military man in my life. There were certainly a lot of career military who had second careers at Christchurch, both as enlisted and as officer background.

There were two other driving influences. I graduated in 1966 and the Vietnam War was raging on. My older brother[100] had done NROTC and had gone into the Navy from UVA. He was in the Navy Reserve in a recruiting capacity and he did me a great favor. He basically marched his little brother down to the recruiting office in Lynchburg, Virginia, and got me into the pipeline for the Reserve Officer Candidate [ROC] program. That allowed me to take a test, and if you passed the test, it allowed you to go to officer candidate school and get your commission in two summer sessions. Then you were in the Navy—contingent upon your graduating from college. Otherwise you went in as a seaman recruit. The thing that my brother did for me that was so nice and I didn't appreciate it at the time, because I was skeptical of anything anyone over thirty told me—I really didn't want to join the Navy, and I only did it because my brother made me do it, but it gave me longevity credit.[101] I raised my right hand in 1968. I graduated from college in 1970. I had two years longevity on any other ensign. I got my commission in October 1970 and I was already in the top of my pay grade. That stayed with me all the way through for thirty-two years. That was why I got thirty-two years, for as an O-6 you have to retire after thirty years, but I had two years enlisted service. I made more money than the commanding officer of my ship, when my divers pay and my longevity were combined.

First I went to the Naval School, Diving and Salvage, which was then at the Washington Navy Yard. I went through in the winter, and it was cold. I graduated in May 1971 and was stationed on a ship out of San Diego, California. I reported to the ship and promptly went on a four-month cruise in-country in Vietnam. This was [on board] USS *Sioux*, an ATF, an oceangoing tug and salvage ship no longer around. They were a wonderful class of ships that were named after Native American tribes—the *Apache*, *Ute*, *Seneca* and so forth. The *Sioux* took me around the world for the three years I was on that ship. I started at the bottom as an ensign who barely knew the pointy end of the ship. I was communications officer and operations officer; actually I think it was communications officer/ first lieutenant, and thank God I had a chief warrant officer [boatswain] who knew what he was doing. Ultimately, I became executive officer, and the ship was sold to the Turks and I was the officer-in-charge of the ship to take it to Turkey. I had five American sailors as my team and sixty Turkish sailors as my "charges," and my job was to make sure they got to Turkey safely. It took three and a half months. The journey was from San Diego through the Panama Canal, up the Sabine River to Orange, Texas. We gave them a barracks barge and we towed the barracks by way of San Juan, Puerto Rico to Spain, across the Mediterranean to Gölcük near Istanbul. The actual transit was probably about one and a half to two months, and the rest of the time was fixing things we broke.

In Vietnam, my biggest duty was to raise a freighter in a harbor town named Qui Nhon. This was a freighter named the SS *Green Bay*, which was loaded with retrograde U.S. Army gear—this was 1972—and we were winding down a bit. The ship was fully loaded and was sunk alongside the pier by an enemy swimmer.[102] We spent two and a half months to unload the ship, right the ship, patch the holes, pump it out and tow it out of there. It was hazardous, because there was enemy action in the area around. We had to leave the harbor every night to avoid being shot at and steam around in circles and come in at the crack of dawn the next morning and set up work. It was exhausting, and the other part of the job was raising boats in the river that fed the port, and I was in Vietnam for four months. We operated up and down the coast and relocated POL [petroleum oil lubricants] docking buoys, which involved using explosives to relocate the huge chains. I was never shot at in anger. You could hear the bombs and explosions in the background, and I feel very fortunate in comparison to some of my contemporaries.[103]

Communal living at Christchurch and in the military

Communal living is a maturing experience, and on a small ship in the Navy, you live in close quarters, and on a salvage ship, there are five officers and sixty men and there is very little formality. You are close to a wide range of people from all walks of life. You are literally in the same boat, and I think that Christchurch gave me that sense that there is worth in everybody and everyone has a role.

In terms of leadership, both at Christchurch and in the Navy, it is your job as a leader to bring out the best in the people who work for you. Captain Riley was a towering figure, like my father, but it was his title of respect that impressed me. The enforcement of discipline at school was, in all honesty, not important. I was probably something of a wuss. I didn't push the limits too much. I was young, I was malleable and I was immature. Only a little of that went away in college. A whole lot of it went away in the Navy. I volunteered to be a diver. I was given the opportunity to pick a job, which is ridiculous because the Navy is going to give you whatever job they need you to do. There was a shaft of light pointing to a poster of a guy in a diving hardhat. I thought it was cool, and I found out I could be on small, non-combatant ships. It was serendipitous and fine, for it put me with some of the finest individuals I could possibly be with from all walks of life—officer and enlisted. The training is arduous and tests your physical and mental strength—the discipline of being on board ship and that period in Vietnam where you are exhausted and are trying to get your job done. The neat thing, and I think this would appeal to Christchurch boys, is that you have a tremendous amount of responsibility if you are a junior officer, particularly if you are on a small ship—you are a department head, and you have a crew of men who work for you. As you become more proficient, you become an underway officer of the deck. You are the captain's agent during your watch, and you are responsible for the safety of the ship in all aspects. It is a big deal.

Personal development at school and in the military

Bob Yarbrough was more of an intellectual and led from the strength of his intellectual ability. I don't think there is anyone who went to Christchurch during his tenure who doesn't remember the Word of the Day, and to this very day I still know what an "auspicious occasion" is and where the origins of "trivia" come from. In terms of relating that to the Navy, it is simply the hierarchical structure: Bob Yarbrough was the captain of the ship. In the salvage navy, the people who make it work are the senior enlisted. When I first reported to my ship, the commanding officer [CO] was a lieutenant commander Limited Duty Officer [LDO] who had come up through the ranks. That man could part the waters. He was a bit rough around the edges, but he could do anything. The second CO was only a few years older than me and a graduate of the U.S. Naval Academy and simply lacked the gravitas of experience and age. He was well trained but wasn't the same as Captain Sorenson, who was a seaman.

The Christchurch experience and military life

The aspects of communal living and a hierarchical structure—teachers and administrators—are present. You and your classmates and you and your athletic team are the sailors on that little boat, also known as the school. Another thing I admired was the sort of can-do attitude. Christchurch was not a rich school and it did not have a lot of frills that particularly wealthy schools today have. School administrators were very much conscious of that and wanted to take care of the facility. We had work periods where you had to clean up the classrooms and clean up the building. It was a serious disciplinary offense if you spoiled something with graffiti or left trash mess or something like that. That sense of caring for your space, taking ownership of the space where you are, certainly translates to life aboard ship in the Navy. These are things shared by both the school and the Navy. In one sense, the experiences were seemingly a bit peculiar. Christchurch of that era was an all-male environment, and college at Hampden-Sydney was all male, and I went into what was then an all-male environment in the diving navy then. There was at Christchurch a "male camaraderie" that enables people to get along with other guys and live with a kind of crudity that can sometimes arise in both environments.

On the observation by Vice Admiral John W. Craine, Jr., '64, USN (Ret.), that at Christchurch and in the armed forces one is judged not "by who you are but what you are"

John is absolutely correct. Particularly in the salvage navy, all jobs are important, and there is no distinction in the importance of various jobs or the skill shown by the entire crew. At school, there were some people who were outstanding, such as Bob Yarbrough, and others in the community who were not and did not contribute to the community. We talked earlier about academics and athletics at Christchurch. Christchurch gave me the opportunity to discover what I was good at. I was lousy at baseball. I never tried basketball, though I was tall. I liked soccer, but I was never very good at it. But I finally discovered one day that I could run forever, and I became a cross-country runner, and in spring track I became a two-miler and a miler. The success I was encouraged to develop in myself as an athlete—in the running aspect at least—gave me the confidence later on, and when I was wondering what I was going to do in my Navy career and volunteered to go into the diving world, which was also physical, I had confidence in my physical abilities at that point. It certainly started at Christchurch by being a member of the track team.

Lieutenant Colonel James Boyd Spencer '66
U.S. Army (Cold War era/War on Terror)

Boyd Spencer had a fine career at Christchurch, becoming vice president of the choir and a prefect, assuming what the 1966 *Tides* calls "hegemony over the residents of the white house."[104] He graduated from the University of the South in Sewanee, Tennessee, and later enrolled in the University of Richmond, from which he earned a master's degree in the summer of 1972. He was the first two-year Army Reserve Officers Training Corps graduate there. He was commissioned in late summer of 1972 as the Vietnam War was ending, and he reported to Armor School at Fort Knox, Kentucky, for branch training and what he assumed would be ultimate assignment to Vietnam. This did not materialize, as the armed forces were being reduced in wake of the Vietnamization program, wherein combat assignments in the Republic of Vietnam were being turned over in entirety to the government of South Vietnam.

Following his release from active duty, he began a career in educational development activity and has gone on to posts in the academic world, including working under the tutelage of David Charlton, dean of church schools in the diocese of Virginia. He has pursued a dual career, rising to increasingly responsible positions in the U.S. Army Reserve, which included extended recalls to active duty during the First Gulf War and in support of NATO operations in Bosnia. His competence and skill as an Army officer is evidenced by the fact that he was as a reserve officer given command of a team of multiservice, multinational members training others for deployment to the Balkans. His final assignment in the Army Reserve was to teach ROTC students at Hampton University, a preeminently excellent, historically black college, and he reflects that he considers himself a "son of Hampton."

Coming to Christchurch

I was growing up in Old Church, Virginia, in rural Hanover County as the only child of two reserved parents. My father was a physician, my mother a college professor. Both were veterans of World War II. My father flew twenty-five missions over Germany in a B-17. My mother served in the WAVES.[105] One of my father's medical partners had sent both of his sons to Christchurch, and they had had good experiences. Knowing that boys need the companionship of other boys and the mentoring of more than one man, my father asked me during my eighth year if I would like to go to boarding school at Christchurch. I was delighted at the prospect and said yes.

Significant influences at school

Colonel Nunn, Captain Riley and Commander Smart [Chaplain Corps, USN] were three of the most important influences on my life at Christchurch, though all the masters that I met there had an influence on me, each in his own way. These three men, all retired military, were the most influential. They personified for me the values of duty, honor and country. Those values came together in the context of a small community, informed and shaped by Anglican tradition. The Episcopal Church was central to my Christchurch experience. One upperclassman was particularly influential in my experience, and that was Joe Farrar.[106] He was the natural leader of the school, the best athlete any of us had ever seen. Yet at a time when there was institutionalized hazing of younger boys by older boys in all southern prep schools, he treated everyone with dignity. He went on to serve with distinction in the Army Special Forces in Vietnam. Though we were not at the time close, he became for me a role model that served me well during my military career.

Choosing the armed forces

I graduated from Sewanee in June 1970 and five days later reported to Fort Knox, Kentucky, for the basic six weeks ROTC summer camp, which is a prerequisite to enroll in the senior ROTC. I was the first two-year ROTC cadet at the University of Richmond. I received a master's degree there and was commissioned a second lieutenant in the summer of 1972. Vietnam was winding down. Most of us who were placed in the combat arms were put on orders for MACV [Military Assistance Command Vietnam]. I reported that October to the U.S. Army Armor School at Fort Knox for the Armor Basic Officer Leaders Course and then the cavalry and recon scout modules in preparation for deployment as an advisor to the ARVN [Army of Vietnam] forces . . . In early 1973 I got off a helo in a snowstorm with my six-man team, was trucked back to our AO and informed that none of us were going to Vietnam. We were being reassigned. We were asked for our preferences and I requested one of our armor brigades in Europe. In typical Army fashion, I was assigned to the 6th Cavalry Regiment at Fort Meade, MD, as a platoon leader. I reported in on Friday and was told to come back Monday. That Sunday, the Washington papers announced that the 6th Cavalry was being moved to Texas. On Monday, I was reassigned to something called the Office of the Secretary of Defense Test 4 at First Army headquarters.

Service history in the military

My introduction to the Army I have come to know and love began Tuesday morning, when I marched into the adjutant's office and reported in. I was told to walk down a long hall, knock and report in to Colonel H. T. "Smokey" Matthews, an Army legend. He was a tough old infantry officer with ribbons up to his epaulets, U.S. Army Air Corps Glider wings from WWII, the Big One, and two stars on his Combat Infantryman's Badge. I dutifully knocked, heard the command from the other side of the door, "Come in," marched in, came to attention while looking six inches over the commander's head while barking, "Sir, Spencer, James B., 2nd Lieutenant, reporting for duty." Colonel Matthews fixed me with a look of horror and left me standing there at attention for twenty seconds, which seemed like ten minutes. Then he barked to his adjutant, "Harvey, there is a Cavalry second lieutenant in my office and how in the hell did he get here?" Major Harvey yelled down the hall, "I don't know sir, he must have snuck in." At that point, still at attention and saluting, I requested permission to withdraw. In about another twenty seconds, the major, sergeant major and a captain walked in, and with Colonel Matthews they all started to laugh. Colonel Matthews said, "Son, you are supposed to be Special Forces captain, not a Cavalry second lieutenant." I told him that, be as it may, that was what I was. What followed was the best two years of my career, knee deep with talented but irreverent warriors right back from Vietnam.

That afternoon, the Special Forces captain arrived, an Airborne Ranger straight off the plane from Vietnam and commanding an A Team. He sported a West Point ring and hair over his collar and no name tag. He said he knew his name, didn't have to check it to remember it and had learned how to spell it as a student at the Trade School on the Hudson. He became my roommate, and life was good. I had been taken in to the best, most depraved fraternity at Fort Meade. No one, but no one, was going to mess with their second lieutenant. Later I went to the officers' club and ran into 2nd Lieutenant Gugy Irving '67, USAF, who was assigned on the National Security Agency side of Fort Meade with spies and spooks. I didn't know what he did, but he said it was legal. As you know, the NSA has certain intelligence functions, such as listening to communications, that would be considered eavesdropping.

I did my two years of active duty at Fort Meade, Fort Campbell and Camp

[Fort] Drum, then returned to a position in development at Randolph-Macon and career in the Army Reserve. I spent ten years in the 80th Division as a training officer and operations officer of one of the battalions. My wife, Lois, and I moved to Jackson, Mississippi, where I became chief development officer for Millsaps College, Bob Yarbrough's alma mater. I joined the 2nd Maneuver Training Command, which trained and tested units with a jungle warfare mission. We would wake up on Friday mornings, work a couple of hours, and then I would fly to Jacksonville, Florida, with my team. We'd board Hueys [UH1 helicopters] for a couple of days as an advisor with a group lost in the jungle.

I was promoted to major and went to 87th Maneuver Area Command in Birmingham, Alabama, and at the same time went to Sewanee as chief development officer. [I] then went to the 100th Division and was executive officer of an armor battalion. I was there when a task force from the division was called to active duty for Desert Storm, the first war in the Gulf. I mobilized at Fort Knox, where we prepared ten million dollars worth of tank ammo to destroy the Republican Guard but never got out of the country until the War was over. Sometime later David Charlton[107] entered my life and invited me back to Virginia for a decade in the church schools organization.

In the Army Reserve I worked in the First Army Emergency Operations Center as a watch officer, and served a tour in the U.S. Joint Forces Command [USJFCOM][108] at Norfolk as a combat arms division team chief. At that time, the commander of USJFCOM was also North Atlantic Treaty Organization commander on this side of the pond. One day I was sitting in a church school's car in North Carolina waiting to see an educational consultant on behalf of Christchurch School when I got a call on my cell phone advising that I was being recalled to active duty for one year to support NATO operations in Bosnia. I was told to pull my team together and report to the naval base at Norfolk, Virginia, for further assignment to Fort Benning, Georgia. I was there for three months with my team, comprised of officers from all services plus two Brits and a Canadian. We were training personnel deploying to the NATO or Joint Headquarters in the Balkans. When we got back to Norfolk, my boss, a marine brigadier general, sent me to SETAF[109] in Vicenza, Italy, as a reward for not having presided over disasters downrange at Fort Benning. This was the first time JFCOM had ever deployed a JTF [Joint Task Force] downrange under the command of a reserve officer. They even gave me a medal. Most guys get medals for doing something heroic. I got one for not fouling up at Fort Benning and embarrassing the command in Norfolk. My final tour was as the Reserve Battalion Commander and Assistant Professor of Military Science at Hampton University. I taught the capstone course for senior ROTC cadets ... Hampton and Howard are the Ivy League of the historically black colleges and universities. It was an interesting tour, teaching second and third generation Hamptonians. As a former member of the faculty I discovered that I, too, am considered a Hamptonian by the university. Along with Christchurch, Sewanee and Richmond, I count myself as one of her sons.

I retired as a lieutenant colonel in July 2000, thirty years and thirty days from the date I reported to Fort Knox for basic training. On the Army side of the house, when one hits sixty, the suffix "Reserve" disappears and one becomes United States Army, (Retired). It has been a wonderful career and a life-changing experience. I was hesitant to do this oral history, feeling somehow that my modest story doesn't belong in the same book with guys like Joe Farrar,[110] John Craine,[111] and Pinky Henderson,[112] but my old friend Sandy Monroe[113] asked me to do it and it has turned out to be an opportunity to relive what has been the best part of my professional life.

Communal living at Christchurch and in the military

When I matriculated at Christchurch, the entire student body lived in Bishop Brown, for the most part in cubicles. My first room was a six-man cubicle on the first floor, which held the last six names alphabetically in the freshman class. The life in an Army barracks struck me as nothing out of the ordinary. Christchurch and the Army both placed a premium on self-reliance. Winston Churchill once said that England won her wars on the playing fields of Eton. Athletic fields at Christchurch prepared me well for what the Army was all about. We trained and played as a team in both places, and in each institution, leaders were expected to take care of the men under them and not eat first. I have always had a pretty high degree of self-discipline. The enforcement of discipline at Christchurch was the enforcement of the natural order of things. I viewed discipline in the Army in the same way.

Personal development at school and in the military

A hallmark of the Christchurch faculty during my four years at the school was the modeling of behavior. The men I most admired—Colonel Nunn, Captain Riley, Chaplain Smart [Commander, Chaplain Corps, USN], Dick "Rock" Poulson—didn't just tell us how to speak, dress or act, they showed us. Gentlemen don't lie, cheat or steal. Neither do Army officers. Gentlemen understand sin, confession, forgiveness, redemption and amendment of life. These are helpful concepts in dealing with an eighteen-year-old E-2, away from home for the first time and trying to sort out where his place is in the world. They are also useful in helping a twenty-two-year old second lieutenant. Though he is indeed responsible for everything that goes on or fails to go on in his unit, stuff happens. Chaos is everywhere. Moral courage is telling the "old man" when your unit has a problem or you made a bad call. Bad news doesn't get better with time. Being part of a team means we are all in it together. Loyalty upward and downward builds cohesion. The captain of a Christchurch team down on points understands this. It's no time for excuses. Likewise, Army officers are taught that when things start to fall apart their job is to bring order out of chaos and to exude confidence. I recall Howard Soucek '66, who captained most of the teams upon which I played. He didn't tell teammates what to do; he showed them.

The Christchurch experience and military life

Christchurch was remarkable in that we were all equal. We got the same allowance. We were all treated the same way by "the powers that be." We all lived under the same honor system, and were expected to live by the same code of conduct and suffered the same consequences if we failed to "roger up." It was the same in the Army. At Christchurch we were all students. In the Army we were all green.

On the observation by Vice Admiral John W. Craine, Jr., '64, USN (Ret.), that at Christchurch and the armed forces you are judged not "by who you are but what you are"

Christchurch handed each new student a blank slate. He was free to make of it what he wished. The Army was much the same. No one in the Army knew or cared where you came from. Your first day in the Army was the first day of the rest of your life. When you transferred to a new command, you had to "prove yourself" anew. One bad officer efficiency report [OER] in the Army could end a career. You had to figure out what success looked like and make it happen. Loyalty up, loyalty down was critical. If you took care of your men, they would take care of you. If you took care of your boss, he would take care of you. Some guys never figure that out. I watched an Army brigadier general at Joint Forces Command get relieved and forced into early retirement during the Bosnia intervention because he did not understand that when one fails to practice loyalty down, you have broken faith with the system. This means you are not practicing loyalty up because if you are not practicing loyalty downward, you are not taking care of your boss. I saw this happen at Christchurch a time or two. To be successful at Christchurch—or in the Army—you are required to be a team player. If you can't play team ball, you're outta here.

LIEUTENANT COLONEL GUGY A. IRVING '67
U.S. AIR FORCE
(Vietnam War/Cold War era and First Gulf War)

Gugy Irving ran track and was co-captain of the cross-country team his senior year. He was a volunteer bus driver his last year and reports that he never had to worry about getting a seat. He earned a B.S. from Hobart College in 1971, an M.A. from Central Michigan University in 1976 and a J.D. from George Mason University in 1982. They were earned in night school while he was on active duty and working during the day. He was commissioned a second lieutenant in the last Air Force ROTC class at Hobart. During his student days, the ROTC building was fire bombed in 1970, and that news made *TIME* magazine due to involvement of local police in a mistimed sting operation.[114] His career area was personnel/administrative and he retired in 1991 as a non-rated squadron commander with twenty years service. After retirement he passed the District of Columbia bar examination on the first try and became a United States Criminal Justice Act public defender. He has served on several boards, including eight years on the Christchurch School Board. He was commodore of the Tred Avon Yacht Club in 2010 and is now president of the U.S. Navy League, Eastern Shore Chapter. He has run for elective office, coming within fifty-seven votes of 25,000 total cast for a probate court judgeship. He is the father of one daughter, who attends the University of Texas, class of 2014.

Coming to Christchurch

I was raised as an Episcopalian on the Eastern Shore of Maryland, and our rector's son [Richard Goodwin '63] was at Christchurch. I was not the best student, and I think my parents and I knew that I needed the small classes and personal attention that are the hallmark of Christchurch. Christchurch was the only school I applied to.

Significant influences at school

There were many significant figures and I think the two standouts for me were retired Army Colonel Nunn, my soccer coach, and retired U.S. Navy Captain Riley, my long-suffering math teacher. Both men genuinely cared for their students. I was on the soccer team in college and luckily I was able to avoid most math in college.

Choosing the armed forces

My father had been a Coast Artillery officer in World War I. I was facing the draft and it was a foregone conclusion that I would have to serve, and I wanted to be an officer. My college had only Air Force ROTC so that is what I did. In hindsight, I think I really would have enjoyed being a Coast Guard or Navy officer, as I grew up on the water and have always been a recreational boater.

Service history in the military

My time in the Air Force took me first to a mountaintop radar station above San Jose, California for the first two years where I was one of five assigned officers . . . Then I asked for and got stationed in Maryland, where I was one of the personnel officers for the 1,500 Air Force personnel assigned at National Security Agency. I was granted top secret [TS] security clearance and had that until I retired. While I was not an intelligence officer, I was active on the Fort Meade Junior Officer Council and learned a lot about intelligence gathering. I was next assigned to Bolling Air Force Base in D.C., where I was computer programmer in a detachment of the Air Force Personnel Center at San Antonio, Texas. Then I went to Fort McNair at the National Defense University, where I supervised personnel specialists from all the services and civilians as well. My boss wasn't one of my huge fans, and I saw a quick exit was in order. I called the assignment folks in Texas and as luck would have it, there was a captain's slot in the Pentagon that called for a TS clearance. I was interviewed by a lieutenant colonel and the luck continued. He was a sailor and graduate of my small college and its ROTC unit.

I really liked the Pentagon and worked with the Joint Chiefs of Staff [JCS] personnel shop. I also watched over Air Force people who were assigned outside the Air Force. One was the physician assigned to the Vice President Bush. I got to eat in the White House mess one time. I also had accountability for the Air Force astronauts and made sure that NASA [National Aeronautics and Space Administration] got properly billed for their services. My only overseas assignment was to Incirlik Air Base, Adana, Turkey, as the number two personnel officer, newly promoted to major. The Turks really liked us and were eager to practice English. From there I went to headquarters of the Air Mobility Command [formerly known as the Military Airlift Command] at Scott Air Force Base, near St. Louis.

The good thing was visiting subordinate commands in Europe, the Far East and the United States. My last job came as I pinned on lieutenant colonel, and I was sent to Myrtle Beach, South Carolina, as the senior personnel officer. When I was there, the job was upgraded to a commander's position, and I assumed many support functions, in addition to personnel functions. We sent two of our three flying squadrons to the First Gulf War. It was a busy time for those of us who stayed behind and for a brief time I was what the Air Force used to call a base commander. I retired, perhaps too early, before coming before the colonel promotion board, but I wanted to use my law degree.

Communal living at Christchurch and in the military

I had never thought of the communal aspect of boarding school and how it affected me until this question. My only summer camp saw us cadets living in a former SAC [Strategic Air Command] underground alert facility, where the bomber crews used to run up ramps to the waiting aircraft. I guess dormitory life helped, as I had no problems. I think I might have had a door on the four-man room for this was "living large," compared to the cubicles.[115] I do know that when I was living in California on my first assignment, some of the officers shared off-base apartments. I also lived off base and had no desire for any roomies. I think the honor system at Christchurch was very good preparation for becoming a military officer.

Personal development at school and in the military

I don't think I can isolate my time at Christchurch or at elementary school or at college. I say what Breck Montague has said about Bob Yarbrough's Word of the Day.[116] In fact we had one-day-a-week vocabulary class, and despite the fact that I was not the best student, the foundation has stayed with me and as a psychology major I took the Miller Analogy Test and knocked it out of the ball park. I recall one student who transferred in actually took the dictionary and read it! I think he knew every word.

The Christchurch experience and military life

I can't say that one experience drove the other. I knew I needed Christchurch in order to get into college, but my time was not always fun. I know the boarding school experience got me through college despite the drinking age in New York of eighteen and having females in class. The new policy of having full coeducation is a good one.

LIEUTENANT COLONEL MARK P. VAKOS '82
U.S. Army (Cold War era/War on Terror)

Mark Vakos, of Virginia Beach, Virginia, entered Christchurch in 1980 after spending two years at the Hargrave Military Academy. His uncle and his cousin are graduates of the school. During his time at Christchurch, he served in leadership positions as a proctor and also as a member of the honor council. He graduated in 1982 and enrolled in Lynchburg College, from which he earned a B.A. degree in 1986. Following college graduation, he enlisted in the United States Army and became a scout and has advanced to the rank of lieutenant colonel. He served in support of Operation Just Cause in Panama and in the First Gulf War, known as Desert Storm, and also in Iraqi Freedom. He was selected for officer candidate school and commissioned as an artillery officer. He has earned the following personal awards: Defense Meritorious Service Medal, Meritorious Service Medal (Army), Joint Services Commendation Medal, Army Commendation Medal, Army Achievement Medal, Southwest Asia Service Medal, among others. After about ten years' active service, he transferred to the Army Reserve. In civilian life, he is a civil service employee of the U.S. Army Intelligence and Security Command at Fort Belvoir, Virginia.

Coming to Christchurch

I had two family members who attended and graduated from Christchurch: Robert "Bobby" Vakos '68, an uncle; and a cousin, George Vakos '79. Through them I knew how nice the school was and wanted to attend.

Significant influences at school

The most significant were the chaplain, The Reverend Edward M. "Pope" Gregory; Ben Boneventura, the dean; and Dean Hundley. While I was close to all of them, Dean and I were very close because he was also my advisor. All of them encouraged me to be or do something great with my life. They taught me that it was okay to express and be myself, and that really got me to open up and mature.

Choosing the armed forces

I joined the U.S. Army mostly because I had attended Hargrave Military Academy prior to coming to Christchurch, where I had had a great experience. Also, because all of my friends were going into the Navy, I wanted to do something different. I reached a point, shortly after graduating from college, where I had no discipline or focus. I just wanted to have fun. I often thought about my years at Christchurch and what I learned from wanting to do something with my life. I asked myself why I had not up to this point, and determined what I lacked was self-discipline, which is critical to being an achiever. As I thought it through, I remembered that the military academy was the one place where I had learned and embraced self-discipline, and thus the Army was the place where I would regain it. While at Christchurch, the significant individuals noted above had often commented on the maturity I had developed in the academy and how it enabled me to become the president of student activities, an honor council member and proctor. This I interpreted as confirming my decision to enter the service, specifically the U.S. Army.

Service history in the military

I initially enlisted as a 19D-cavalry scout. While entering as a commissioned officer was an option, I chose to enlist because I needed to relearn how to be responsible and disciplined. Without that, I could not in good conscience lead others. I also wanted to jump out of airplanes and get "hoooah"[117] with the troops, and I didn't think being an officer would allow me to do that. As I completed Advanced Armor Training in 1989, operations in Panama were kicking off and I found myself in a support role there with USSOUTHCOM.[118] I was then assigned to the 1st of the 1st Cavalry, 1st Armored Division in Ansbach Germany, the oldest and most decorated command in the U.S. Army. Within twelve months, I found myself on the ground in Iraq, doing what scouts do, with the mission of countering Saddam Hussein's mischief. I have many stories about what happened there, but it would take days to write it all down.

Being a scout with a reputation, I was selected by the division commander and chief of staff to spearhead in with the division in an HMMWV,[119] carrying the 1st Armored Division chief of staff. He was to be the eyes on the ground while the division commander, Major General Griffith, was in the air above, directing the battle. Cavalry always being out front, the 2nd Armored Cavalry Regiment and the 1st of the 1st Cavalry Regiment formed two echelons and roared across the desert in a blaze of glory with me in an HMMWV between the ranks. It scared the heck out of me, with no armor and a pack of hungry wolves around us shooting anything that moved! For the next seventy-two hours, the chief of staff and I had quite an adventure. When it was over, the commanding general and the chief of staff advised me that they were sending me to officers candidate school [OCS] because they needed more soldiers like me out in front. It would seem that despite my best efforts to remain in enlisted ranks, I would become a commissioned officer anyway.

In September, after nine months of pure hell, I was commissioned a second lieutenant in the intelligence branch of the Army. I would find myself back in Iraq a couple of more times. My last tour ended in April 2007, and no, I am not real crazy about the Middle East.

Communal living at Christchurch and the military

I didn't realize there was no difference between living in the dorms and living in the barracks. Rules are rules and they are in place and enforced for a good reason. Both the Army and Christchurch were rich learning environments, and they just have different curricula. Christchurch definitely prepared me for the road ahead and gave me the foundation I needed to acclimate into the Army environment. As for the enforcement of discipline, I daresay that the "cost" of breaking the rules is harder in the Army but no more so than with any professional career. The biggest penalty is the damage to your reputation; this was etched in my mind at Christchurch. As I served on the honor council, I witnessed firsthand the damage caused by someone's lack of good judgment and the impact it had on the rest of the students. Both the Army and Christchurch have high standards, and they are echoed constantly as a reminder to maintain or exceed them.

Personal development at school and in the military

The significant individuals at Christchurch all had unique personalities. The one thing they all had in common was the push to get everyone to achieve, to set achievable goals. One would do it through sports, the other through religion, academics or social skills. Collectively they were the personality.

Much is the same in the Army. No individual or group of individuals makes up the whole. As you realize this, that is when you begin to understand life and how to steer your ship within the armada. I would say that the difference is in timing, specifically the age I was when I was at Christchurch. Being young and malleable, it only required that a mentor embrace me and teach me that which I needed to learn. My significant individuals at Christchurch did just that for me. Had I not been taught, my integration into the Army and the success I have achieved would have been difficult to achieve, if at all. Dean Hundley perhaps had the greatest influence on me. He spoke to me on my level and eventually bought me up to his. He gave me the courage and desire to embrace the world and live my life.

The Christchurch experience and military life

In many ways my experiences at Christchurch were mimicked throughout my military career and life in general. I was once told that everything you needed to know in life you learned in kindergarten—play nice with others, don't pee in the sandbox, nap when you need to, eat right, listen to the teacher, etc. Well I would change that to "everything you needed to know in life, you learned at Christchurch." I was something of a social introvert. Christchurch brought me out of my shell and taught me how to experience life and interact with others and helped define who I was. It is at this stage that you start to etch in stone your values and begin to set your great expectations. Without the right environment and experiences, it is easy to go down the wrong path. As I was entrusted with various responsibilities such as president of student activities and honor council member, I learned to be a leader and to set high standards. Had I not experienced this, I doubt I'd have gotten this far in the military.

Lieutenant Meredith D. Adkins '00
U.S. Navy (War on Terror/Humanitarian Assistance era)

Lieutenant Adkins, a member of the Class of 2000, was an accomplished athlete and strong citizen of Christchurch. She was, at various points in her time as a student, a prefect, a member of the honor council, a member of the National Honor Society and a member of both the varsity field hockey team and crew. She graduated from the United States Naval Academy and was assigned to the USS *Bataan* (LHD-5), homeported at U.S. Naval Base, Norfolk, Virginia, where she served as division officer for Operations Specialists and Electronic Technicians and was an underway officer of the deck and Surface Warfare Officer. She also served in the Operations Department of Expeditionary Strike Group Two based ashore at Little Creek, Virginia, and in the Public Affairs Office of the Commander, Surface Force, U.S. Atlantic Fleet at U.S. Naval Base Norfolk.

Coming to Christchurch

My mom has been a teacher at Christchurch for twenty-five to twenty-six years now, and I was a little girl running around the Christchurch campus. When I was an eighth grader, my older sister and my younger brother had come here. That's why we came. My mom was teaching here. Halfway through my eighth grade year, David Charlton became acting headmaster. He was named headmaster later. Jack Blair was headmaster for about six months of my eighth grade year.

Significant influences at school

Mr. Todd was probably very influential, and he was a math teacher and academic dean at the time. I am a math person, always have been and always will be. He was influential in academics. Tim O'Keefe was my crew coach and got me interested in the sport and was my adviser. Al Caderet was also my adviser until he left. I still talk to him a lot about the Navy because his father was in it. Probably Doug McMinn was one of my favorite teachers. When I got into the Naval Academy, outside of my mom, he was one of the people here who was most excited for me.

Choosing the armed forces

When I was five years old, I saw the movie *Top Gun*. I wanted to be a fighter pilot. I wanted to be "Maverick," and my mom was teaching here at the time, and a teacher who was here at the time, "Tank" Schroeder, Captain William Schroeder, U.S. Navy—he knew I wanted to be a pilot in the Navy and he had been a pilot in the Navy. We would sit and talk about different airplanes and about the Navy. He told me the place to go if I wanted to be a Navy pilot was the Naval Academy. We would always talk about the Academy and flying, and I remember at the end of my junior year at Christchurch I just got accepted to the Summer Seminar at the Naval Academy, and the first person I wanted to tell was Tank. I called him up. He couldn't have been prouder. Actually, that was the last time I got to talk to him. He died that year.

Service history in the military

I was on the *Bataan* [LHD-5]. I don't think the ship ever went to anyplace too dangerous. I did go to Panama and did some exercises. I was qualified as an underway OOD [officer of the deck]. I left the ship right before they deployed to the Middle East. The Hurricane Katrina deployment was unusual, especially looking back on it, as we were coming back from our exercises in Panama.[120] We had just visited in Texas, at the naval station at Ingleside.[121] We had delivered some helicopters when they said, "There's a big storm coming up the Gulf and we want you guys to stay." We actually came out of Ingleside and followed the hurricane up the Gulf. We were right behind it. It was really scary, the huge waves crashing on the deck.

So the next day we were there. A lot of the helicopters you saw on TV were from *Bataan*.[122] We had planned to go home to Norfolk, and so we didn't have supplies and stuff, so we had to refuel. We were there to be ready, for an LHD has a hospital[123] on board, so we were there if they needed to bring people on board. We could also make our own water. We had a lot of the important players for Katrina come on board and talk to us about what our role was going to be in it. We stayed in the Gulf about three weeks, and at first we were there to help and respond to New Orleans, but later with Gulfport and those places. We had LCACs [Amphibious Air Cushion Craft] embarked, and we were able to be anchored just offshore and took supplies and people to help. We did whatever we could during those three weeks.[124]

We didn't go up the Mississippi. The higher ups on the ship decided that we didn't know the conditions of the Mississippi. There was a little hesitation. We were actually met down there by the USS *Iwo Jima* [LHD-7]. It went up the river, while we helped others. Admiral [Thad W.] Allen[125] and General [Russel L.] Honore[126] came on board—because at first we were the only ship down there—to talk with us and see what we could provide. A couple of days later, the hospital ship the [USNS] *Comfort* [T-AH20] and the USS *Iwo Jima* [LHD-7] came down. We were coming back from being underway for six weeks and we weren't planning on being underway for another three weeks. We pulled a little bit further into the gulf so we could meet up with supply ships.[127]

Communal living at Christchurch and in the military

It was very similar. You're a lot closer. When you go to a public high school, it's a lot different. You only know the people you're really close with or the people you've grown up with. When I came here, you're so close. Girls don't live here, but you're still here for everything, and then you go to the Navy and you live on a ship and you don't have a lot of space to get away from things, but you also have a lot of people who are there if you need them. I liked that. You went to the Naval Academy, and it's very much the same way where you're in close contact with others.

At Christchurch, you are very much held accountable for your actions. Sometimes it's hard for people at Christchurch to get that at first. Little things you might not get into trouble for elsewhere, you do at Christchurch. That's the exact same way it was in the Navy for me. I know when I got to my ship, my division was something of a small group of troublemakers. There were "little things" that they did. That's how it was, you were held responsible for your actions at school, and you were on the ship. For me, it was very similar.

Personal development at school and in the gender-neutral armed forces

They are the same. People always asked how did you deal with it, being a female in the Navy? How did you deal with things? To me it seemed a lot like school here. The higher-up senior officers are a lot like the faculty, and there are some people who are really influential in your life, who help mold you, and then there are some others. Rear Admiral Tyson was probably one of the most influential mentors I had when I was in the Navy. She was a great captain. I talked with her many times when she was captain. She was an inspiration, a mentor. Any time I had a problem I could talk to her. She was very approachable to the females in the wardroom because she had gone up so high. I had the opportunity to see her in the airport a couple of weeks ago.

I just happened to see her, and I said, "You may not remember me," and she said, "Of course I do," and we sat and talked. She asked me how I was doing. It was definitely inspirational. She is the person I'll remember most on the ship and in the Navy. The percentage of women commissioned officers wasn't very high. It became an issue because there weren't a lot of choices you had as far as roommates, and you could get stuck with someone you really didn't mesh with. When I came on board there were only two other female ensigns from my year group. We actually bonded, and I keep in contact with them still.

Personal development at school and in the military

A lot of it was, and perhaps because it's a small school—a lot of the Navy experience is the same. Perhaps it is because there is a small number of females compared to the number of males in the military and here at school. All the students—whatever their gender—are your family. They're there for the good and the bad, and it's very similar in the military. My division was my family, and I took care of them, good and bad. It was very similar to school.

There were a lot of the people in my division who hadn't had the best upbringing. A lot of them got into the Navy to get away from where they had been. It wasn't shocking. It was different, but not shocking to me.

The reason I left *Bataan* was that my knees got bad, and I had to get off the ship. I was with Commander Surface Force Atlantic Fleet [COMNAVSURFLANT] for about a year and then was sent on temporary duty to the staff of Expeditionary Strike Group Two in Little Creek, and I worked in the Operations Department. That was interesting because I had been on the ship where I had done all the exercises, and I went to a position where I was helping to plan all the exercises ships did. I was getting to see a bigger picture. We were the shore controlling command for a lot of the exercises. After that, the whole group was getting ready to move to Bahrain, so I was sent back to COMNAVSURFLANT. I got stationed with the Public Affairs Office. That was a great office. That was interesting, to see things the way staff members see them. There is a different perspective. You see how you dealt with all the things that were happening in the military, the little things that you didn't have to worry about so much when you were on the ship. On the ship you were worried about the operational aspect of things.

My main role at the Public Affairs Office was as coordinator for tours of the ships. It could be anything from a Boy Scout troop to the Chief of Naval Operations [CNO] of Croatia or someone who wanted to tour a ship on the waterfront, and I had to find a ship. A lot of those requests came at the last minute. When a CNO of another country wants to tour a ship, you make it happen. It was very different from what I had started doing, but it was just another part of the Navy puzzle.

I loved the Navy. On a regular schedule, I would be officer of the deck—either in port or underway—and be in charge of the entire ship, which has a thousand people on it. That's very impressive to some people. The other part of it was the people, the people in the military. I loved my divisions. I liked most of the officers. I liked how people worked together to do something that was a lot bigger than they are. You don't realize it while you are doing it.

On the observation by Vice Admiral John W. Craine, Jr., '64, USN (Ret.), that at Christchurch and in the armed forces, you are judged not "by who you are but what you are"

I think that's very true. When I was at Christchurch they did something, and they still do it. You have to give a senior speech. Every senior has to get up and give a senior speech. My senior speech was about how someone different could come to Christchurch and still be accepted. When I went into the Navy, it was very much the same thing. There are people from all different backgrounds. You're working toward a goal together and no one's going to judge you on who you are or where you came from. It's how you go from there. As long as you're helping to get the job done and not hurting, you're treated like another person in the Navy.

When queried about the historic nature of being the first woman to be a qualified presidential pilot in HMX One, Major Jennifer Grieves, USMC observed, "It's not about being a woman, rather it's part of being in an exceptional organization, the United States Marine Corps." Do you feel this applies with equal force to the United States Navy?

I think it does. When you're in, on the ship or something, it's not "You did that well for a woman." You get yelled at, like every other ensign in the ship. You're just another member of the service and it really doesn't matter. The first division I had was probably about seventy-five percent women. Nobody thought this was a bunch of women. It was a bunch of OSs [Operations Specialists]. It's the same for officers. You are not really treated differently, unless you choose to make that an issue. It's not about "I am a pioneering woman." It is rather, "I am an officer in the Navy." Christchurch is very much a family. That's how I saw my ship. You are doing a job. It is very important. It's about the people and that is how Christchurch is. I basically grew up here. I was that little five-year-old kid you saw running around campus. It is about family and that is how I saw my ship, because it is about the people. In the military, if your people aren't happy, if they are in trouble and not doing their job, the big job doesn't get done. It's very much a focus on the people.

Lieutenant Collinson E. P. "Ned" Burgwyn III '04
U.S. Coast Guard (War on Terror)

Lieutenant Burgwyn, an accomplished athlete, is the son of a former Christchurch faculty member. Following graduation, he enrolled in the Virginia Polytechnic and State University and graduated with a B.A. in History in 2008. He was chief justice of the honor court. Following graduation, he entered officer candidate school in the U.S. Coast Guard and upon completion was assigned to CGC *Northland* (WMEC-209), homeported at Portsmouth, as a weapons department officer. The ship participated in counter-narcotics operations in the Caribbean and Eastern Pacific, in Alien Migrant Interdiction Operations (AMIO) and in fisheries protection operations. He was a qualified deck watch officer and a lead boarding officer. He was involved with the repatriation of Cuban/Haitian migrants and search-and-rescue (SAR), one case involving stabilization of a ship foundering in the Atlantic. He has been executive officer of CGC *Mustang* (WPB-1310), a 110-foot cutter in Seward, Alaska. The ship is normally involved with SAR and fisheries protection operations. He is now aide to the commander, First Coast Guard District, in Boston.

Coming to Christchurch School

I was born in Virginia and lived in Williamsburg when I was younger, but in 1998 my family and I moved to Newnan, Georgia, with my father's previous job. During our four years in Georgia, my father got back into teaching/coaching and he looked for a teaching job that would bring us home to Virginia. He found Christchurch, and the summer before my junior year, we moved to Christchurch to live on campus in a faculty house for the next two years. My father taught at Christchurch for six years.

Significant influences at school

I never had my father as a teacher, but he was my baseball coach, lifelong mentor and friend. Donny Pyles was my AP history and Civil War teacher and prepared me for college academics and solidified my decision to pursue a degree in history. I ran my fastest 5k cross-country times under the coaching of Ken Pryzbyl, and Coach A. J. Ruffin pushed me to try indoor track, a sport I would have never considered without his driving us up to Woodberry. Without Jill Shore, I would have never passed calculus and wouldn't have been well enough prepared for the math requirement at Virginia Tech. Mr. Jim Pettyjohn was my advisor for two years and gave me my first experience in political science, a subject in which I pursued a minor.

Choosing the armed forces

Both of my grandfathers were naval officers, one an aviator in World War II and the other a doctor on USS *Leyte* [CV-32] during the Korean War, and I also have ancestors who fought in the Civil War and in World War I. Growing up, I was inspired by their sense of service and started to formulate my ideas about where I could serve best. I originally looked at the Navy, and I joined the Virginia Tech Corps of Cadets, but while in college I realized that in all my time boating and fishing around Tidewater, Virginia, the Coast Guard would be the best place for me. In terms of the school's influence, Christchurch is a place where no student's dreams go unnoticed or unsupported by the faculty. It is such a close community that everyone on campus knows where you want to go to college and what you would like to do afterwards. I never felt lost in the shuffle and received nothing but encouragement to pursue a career in the military.

Service history in the military

My first assignment was aboard the CGC *Northland* [WMEC-209], homeported in Portsmouth, Virginia, where I served as a deck watch officer, the weapons division officer and law enforcement officer for eighteen months. The ship's mission was Maritime Law Enforcement, and I participated in counter-narcotics missions and migrant interdiction operations in the Caribbean and Eastern Pacific. I went to Panama, Colombia and a handful of other Caribbean and South American nations. My proudest participation in dangerous duty was on a sinking commercial fishing boat sixty nautical miles off the coast of Virginia. While on a commercial fisheries enforcement patrol on Northland, we received a call from a vessel taking water on faster than they could pump it overboard. We made best speed for about forty nautical miles to close the distance and render assistance. When we arrived, we found an eighty-foot fishing vessel dead in the water and an HH60 Jayhawk from Air Station Elizabeth City overhead trying to lower down a small gas-powered pump. The fishermen were having trouble keeping the pump going, so I was tasked to be the boarding officer and lead a four-man rescue and assistance team over to help pump the water. We were alongside in just a few minutes, and when I jumped over the rail of the fishing boat from our small boat, water shot from the steering gear room and net locker scuttles straight into the air as the boat rocked in the seas. Both of these spaces were flooded solid and the source of flooding had not been located. As I checked the boat for survival gear and equipment, the engineers from my team got a pump we had brought going and dewatered the boat in less than twenty minutes. Line from a net float had wrapped itself around the rudderposts in the bottom of the hull and had broken the packing that served as the watertight seal where the rudderposts passed through the bottom of the boat. My team was able to repair this and keep the boat from sinking.

I am now[128] in my second assignment, which is executive officer of CGC *Mustang* [WPB-1310], which is a 110-foot patrol boat home-ported in Seward, Alaska. Our mission is search and rescue [SAR] and fisheries enforcement in the Gulf of Alaska. It is a very different job as the crew is only seventeen—two officers and fifteen enlisted—and I am responsible for all of the command's personnel, financial tasks as well as being navigator and lead boarding officer. It is a lot of paperwork, but with such a small crew, I am able to see the outcome of my work every day. Driving a boat in Alaska is also an incredible and sometimes breathtaking experience.

Communal living at Christchurch and in the military

I did not live in the dormitory at Christchurch, but I did live on campus in a faculty house, which oddly enough prepared me for life on board a ship. At Christchurch, work and play happened at the same place, and life on a ship is much the same. Two-month patrols at a time and six months a year at sea blurs the line between work and recreation, and having the experience at Christchurch helped me prepare for the fact that my desk, bed, gym, TV and supervisors were all within the same steel hull.

Serving as a prefect at Christchurch taught me the value of honesty, integrity and character. These are crucial values for serving in the military and especially in tight quarters aboard a ship or boat.

Personal development in the military and at Christchurch

The culture of Christchurch is that hard work and deadlines matter, both of which are crucial in the military. The difference is that a lack of hard work and a missed deadline don't just affect yourself as it does in school but it directly affects the crew that depends on you. In my time in the Coast Guard, I have seen many people who were willing to risk their lives at sea in small rafts to reach our country. Regardless of the immigration debate, it made me realize how lucky Americans are and how fortunate I was to have an upbringing where I never had to worry about the necessities of life.

Vice Admiral John W. Craine, Jr., '64, USN (Ret.), once observed that both in the Navy and at Christchurch you are judged not by who you are but what you are. Do you find that this applies to your service in the U.S. Coast Guard?

In the military, being a nice and likeable guy helps, but does not inspire people to follow you. You must learn and know your field. Doing what is right is seldom the easiest route, but if your crew knows that you do what is right, what defines your decision making, they will follow your example.

EPILOGUE

The recollections are now before us, preserved and withdrawn intact from the memories of those who experienced life along the Rappahannock River. Those who lived here for a time prepared themselves for rich, diverse journeys, lives filled with adventure and service—to their communities and the nation—that would play out over forty to fifty odd years after physically leaving this place behind them. It is frequently said that they return with great regularity, keen anticipation and gusto to see the place that played a central role in their existence and development. It is said that this is just one thing—quite possibly the most distinctive—that sets Christchurch alumni apart, something terribly hard to define or express. In so doing, they are like migratory birds, such as the osprey that leave the river for the winter but return in the warmer spring, strengthened by the lengthy northward journey.

What is it that links the school and the service to the nation?

The answer, which has been demonstrated in what has gone before, is that there were people on the faculty and staff who gave of themselves to help adolescents reach maturity. Their names appear again and again: William Smith, Grover Jones, "Spud" Parker, Gerry Cooper, "Bob A," "Jungle Jim" Taylor, The Colonel, Chaplain Smart, "Rock" Poulson and Fred Riley. The late Colonel Bill Dabney '53, who as a young officer led his Marines to triumph atop Hill 881 at Khe Sanh in 1968, expressed it well. He felt, as he said in his oral history, that what connects the school to the Marine Corps, and in fact to all the uniformed services past and present, is that its leaders have demonstrated the desire to do what they do properly: "They cared." More importantly, they have transmitted to their students the desire to do the same. To borrow and paraphrase from Charles Gibson, an ABC newscaster who described Arlington National Cemetery as "an honored place, beautiful for all that it represents," Christchurch is made the lovelier by the devotion to and love of the place and the country felt by its family members, present and past.

Afterword

They shall grow not old, as we that are left grow old

Age shall not weary them, nor the years condemn

At the going down of the sun and in the morning,
We will remember . . .

Ode to Remembrance
Lawrence Binyon
1914

What you have read was created to give human form and a sense of time and place to the monument from which those who come to Christchurch can view the river and quite possibly have their spirits renewed. To continue the role played by the faculty and staff of the school, a portion of whatever profits might be earned from the sale of the book will be given to the school for financial aid of future students whose family members have served or are presently serving in the uniformed services of the United States.

Appendix A

Christchurch Alumni Veterans

Woodford C. Harwood '23	U.S. Army
Herbert B. Mayers '23	U.S. Army
Edward T. Ryland '23	U.S. Army
John C. Wyllie '24	U.S. Army (AAF)
Charles L. Darbie '26	U.S. Army
Joseph Vandeventer '26	U.S. Army
William C. F. Robards '27	U.S. Navy
Richard J. Bischoff '28	U.S. Army
William P. Jones '28	U.S. Army
Robert W. Smethie '28	U.S. Army (AAF)
Donald W. Wingfield '28	U.S. Navy
John W. Monroe '30	U.S. Army
Frank B. Meacham '30	U.S. Marine Corps
John B. Pinner II '30	U.S. Marine Corps
William J. Gascoyne III '30	U.S. Army
Kingsley Fisher '31	U.S. Army
L. Winder Lane '31	U.S. Army
William A. Pleasants, Jr., '31	U.S. Army
John A. A. Luttrell '31	U.S. Army
Everett L. Blake '32	U.S. Army
Lewis O'Hara '32	U.S Army
Russell Fisher, MD, '32	U.S. Navy
Michael Wheat '32	U.S. Army
Frank Morton '32	U.S. Army
Meredith L. Scott '32	U.S. Navy
Richard Simmonds '32	U.S. Army
Cary B. Adkins '32	U.S. Army
Robert C. Nase '32	U.S. Army
George C. Lockard, Jr., '32	U.S. Army
John R. Henderson '33	U.S. Army

E. Diller Harding '33	U.S. Navy
Thomas S. Marchant '33	U.S. Army (AAF)
Lawrence W. Latane, Jr. '33	U.S. Navy
Nathaniel B. Page '33	U.S. Army
Edward K. Markell, MD, '34	U.S. Navy
Charles B. Leaf '34	U.S. Coast Guard
George A. Hilbert '34	U.S. Army (AAF)
George Adreon '34	U.S. Army
Harry H. Witzke, Jr., '34	U.S. Army
George Upshur Pope '34	U.S. Army
Arthur Sherman '34	U.S. Navy
Joyce C. Gilliam '35	U.S. Army
J. D. Crombie Garrett '35	U.S. Marine Corps
Richie N. Henderson '35 (KIA)	U.S. Navy
Miles A. Libbey, Jr., '35	U.S. Navy
Walter A. Hazelwood '36	U.S. Army
Tazewell McCorkle '36	U.S. Army
David E. Latane '36	U.S. Army (AAF)
Lawrence G. Lewis, Jr., '36	U.S. Army
Sydney A. Vincent '36	U. S. Army
William Vernon Ward '36	U.S. Army
Roland B. Miller '36	U.S. Army
Harry E. Karr, Jr., '36	U.S. Army
Wilson T. Shelton '36	U.S. Army
Thomas R. Slingluff '37	U.S. Army (AAF)
John A. B. Davies '37	U.S. Army
Robert Jones '37 (KIA)	U.S. Army
Thomas D. Martin '37	U.S. Navy
John T. Vance III '38	U.S. Army
Dudley Amoss '38	U.S. Army (AAF)
Cecil W. Page '38	U.S. Army
Stuart J. Fuller '38	U.S. Army (AAF)
Eugene Cassell '38	U.S. Army
Frederick D. Goodwin, Jr., '38	U.S. Navy
Charles E. Ayers '39	U.S. Army
Robert S. Caperton '39	U.S. Army
James L. Chavasse '39	U.S. Army
William A. Fenner '39	U.S. Army
Earnest D. Harding '39	U.S. Army
Roger Moorman '39	U.S. Navy
John H. Norton '39	U.S. Army

William F. Byers '39	U.S. Army
Fielding Greaves '39	U.S. Army
Malcus S. Horton '39	U.S. Air Force
Herbert S. Osborn '39	U.S. Army (AAF)
Jim Dischinger '39	U.S. Army
Thomas G. Jones '39	U.S. Army
William Slate '39	U.S. Army
Wiley P. Ballard, Jr., '40	U.S. Army (AAF)
Segar Hinkle '40	U.S. Army (AAF)
Robert Holloway '40	U.S. Army
Julian W. Clarkson '40	U.S. Navy
Thomas D. Crittenden '40	U.S. Coast Guard
Henry K. Fowle '40	U.S. Navy
Nathaniel Young '40	U.S. Army
Ellis Joyner '40	U.S. Army (AAF)
Thomas A. Devan '40	U.S. Army
Eugene A. Hildreth '41	U.S. Navy
Carroll C. Chowning '41	U.S. Navy
Charles H. Cline '41	U.S. Army
Freeland Mason '41	U.S. Army
Hugh Dischinger '41	U.S. Army (AAF)
Vincent Canby '41	U.S. Navy
Hunter T. Wagener '41	U.S. Army
Charles B. Tebbs '41	U.S. Marine Corps
Catesby T. Field '41	U.S. Army
John M. Perry '42	U.S. Army
Forrest B. Holloway '42	U.S. Army
V. Randolph Chowning '42	U.S. Army (AAF)
James S. G. Davenport '42	U.S. Army
R. Langley-Wood '42	U.S. Navy
William C. Styron '42	U.S. Marine Corps
Thomas P. Peyton III '42	U.S. Marine Corps
William "Mick" Bowman '42	U.S. Army
Eugene Deas '42	U.S. Navy
Robert H. Mumper '42	U.S. Army (AAF)
Britton N. Wagstaff '42	U.S. Army
W. Ray Winder '42	U.S. Army (AAF)
John White Perry '42	U.S. Army
James T. Breckinridge '42	U.S. Marine Corps
Robert M. Treser '42	U.S. Army
Lewis Flemer, Jr., '43	U.S. Army

Chester D. Porter, Jr., '43	U.S. Army
John K. Cowperthwaite '43	U.S. Navy
John Flemer '43	U.S. Army
Thomas Flemer '44	U.S. Army
Edward Von Walter '43	U.S. Navy
Stephen L. Thorne '43	U.S. Army (AAF)
Howard E. Topping '43	U.S. Navy
William C. Vandeburgh '43	U.S. Army
Lewis Cardozo '44 (KIA)	U.S. Marine Corps
Daniel M. Greathead '44	U.S. Army
Joseph Thrift '44 (KIA)	U.S. Army
Jebil Moll '44	U.S. Army (AAF)
H. Waller Whittemore '44	U.S. Navy
Franklin McGinnes '44	U.S. Navy
William C. Hogge '44	U.S. Air Force
George J. Magnus, Sr., '44	U.S. Army (AAF)
Robert B. Lloyd '44	U.S. Army
Jesse W. Topping '45	U.S. Army
William T. Vrooman '45	U.S. Army
A. Wallace Wooten '45	U.S. Army
Powell W. Davis '45	U.S. Army
Richard E. Marshall '45	U.S. Army
Collins Snyder '45	U.S. Navy
William C. Avery '47	U.S. Coast Guard
James M. Miller '47	U.S. Army
John B. Bullard, Jr., '47	U.S. Navy
Frank Churchill '47	U.S. Army
Hodges Gallop '48	U.S. Coast Guard
Byron W. Graves '48	U.S. Army
Robert R. Simmons '49	U.S. Army
A. Daniel Alexis '49	U.S. Navy
David Kippenbrock '49	U.S. Navy
George H. St. Clair '49	U.S. Navy
I. Edward Trotter '49	U.S. Army
L. Ward Edwards '49	U.S. Navy
Robert Chewning '49	U.S. Navy
John W. Rhein '49	U.S. Army
William C. Bryson, Jr., '50	U.S. Marine Corps
Frederick P. Anthony '50	U.S. Marine Corps
Archer Goodwin '50	U.S. Coast Guard
Joseph Eggler '50	U.S. Army

Cuthbert Bristow '50	U.S. Army
William A. Griffin '50	U.S. Navy
Eugene A. Tinsley '51	U.S. Marine Corps
Richard G. Moncure '51	U.S. Air Force
Walter Lord '51	U.S. Army
William H. Street III '52	U.S. Army
Robert L. Montague '52	U.S. Navy
William H. Street III '52	U.S. Army
John G. Pollard III '52	U.S. Army
Silas W. Barnes, Jr., '52	U.S. Army
Frank Willoughby '53	U.S. Air Force
William H. Dabney '53	U.S. Marine Corps
Gerald L. Cooper '53	U.S. Navy
Joel McGurk '53	U.S. Navy
Roy Cather '53	U.S. Army
Henry Eichelberger '54	U.S. Army
Philip H. Wallace '54	U.S. Army
Ed Cather '54	U.S. Navy
Otho L. Gladding III '54	U.S. Army
Charles Wilkins '54	U.S. Air Force
E. Worth Higgins '54	U.S. Army
William C. Tulloss '54	U.S. Army
William M. Ferguson, Jr., '55	U.S. Navy
L. Easley Spencer '55	U.S. Army
Thomas L. Grove '55	U.S. Air Force
John S. Hopewell '56	U.S. Navy
F. H. Daniel Cook '56	U.S. Coast Guard
David Herndon '56	U.S. Coast Guard
Taliaferro Bargamin '56	U.S. Air Force
Jess Hinson '56	U.S. Navy
Horace C. Robison, Jr., MD, '56	U.S. Navy
S. Woodruff Bentley '56	U.S. Air Force
Charles A. Ferguson '56	U.S. Army
Littleton Cockrell '57	U.S Army
Roger Garlow '57	U.S. Coast Guard
Mike Kelly '57	U.S. Marine Corps
Herbert Wolfrey '57	U.S. Army
H. Murrell McLeod '58	U.S. Navy
Mason T. New '58	U.S. Coast Guard
John Stock '58	U.S. Army (NGUS)
Ennolls Stephens '58	U.S. Coast Guard

Owen Bowser '58	U.S. Marine Corps
Gregory F. Smith '58	U.S. Navy
Thomas G. McMillan '59	U.S. Coast Guard
James K. M. Newton III '59	U.S. Marine Corps
H. Thomas Fisher '59	U.S. Coast Guard
John H. Toole '59	U.S. Army
Thomas B. Booth '59	U.S. Navy
Willis B. Ennis '59	U.S. Army
Robert B. Powell '59	U.S. Army
Leavenworth M. Ferrell '59	U.S. Marine Corps
Vance A. Webb '60	U.S. Air Force
F. Davis Drumheller, Jr., '60	U.S. Marine Corps
W. West Foster '60	U.S. Army
Christopher N. Banks '60	U.S. Air Force
Alexander G. Monroe '60	U.S. Navy
George W. Warren IV '60	U.S Army
Nathaniel P. Ward IV '60	U.S. Army
George M. Temple '60	U.S. Marine Corps
William A. B. Thomas '60	U.S. Navy
Ward R. Scull III '61	U.S. Army
Benjamin P. A. Warthen '61	U.S. Army
Robert R. Goodhart '61	U.S. Army
Robert A. McMillan '61	U.S. Navy
Paul F. Judson, Jr., '61	U.S. Air Force
Thomas R. Klingelhoefer '61	U.S. Navy
Beverly R. Tucker, III '61	U.S. Army
G. Garland Jefferson '61	U.S. Army
John J. Ambler, Jr., '62	U.S. Army (NGUS)
Roderic S. Leland '62	U.S. Navy
Richard B. Bowles, MD, '62	U.S. Army
Dunbar Lawson '62	U.S. Navy
David L. Henderson '62	U.S. Army
James D. Enochs, Jr., '62	U.S Marine Corps
Alfred P. Scott '62	U.S. Marine Corps
Willis M. Gregory '62	U.S. Marine Corps
John S. Shaw II '62	U.S. Army
Robert Bozarth '63	U.S. Navy
Lewis B. Puller, Jr., '63	U.S. Marine Corps
Charles C. Tylander '63	U.S. Navy
E. Emery Gray '63	U.S. Army
Robert H. Ball '63	U.S. Marine Corps

John Erich Decher III '63	U.S. Marine Corps
Jon M. Samet, MD, '63	U.S. Army
William R. McLean, MD, '63	U.S. Army
Robert E. Mills '64	U.S. Army
George R. Wood '64	U.S. Marine Corps
Thomas Welsh '64	U.S. Marine Corps
Sterling Bolling '64	U.S. Air Force
John W. Craine, Jr., '64	U.S. Navy
C. Fletcher Flemer III '64	U.S. Army
Ian Refo '64	U.S. Navy
Will J. Wallace III '64	U.S. Marine Corps
David Ware, Jr., '64	U.S. Army
Richard E. Potter '64	U.S. Army
John G. Smart '65	U.S. Army
Tim Tepper '65	U.S. Coast Guard
George R. Scott '65	U.S. Navy
James A. Boone '65	U.S. Army
Patrick D. Thrasher, MD, '65	U.S. Army
Joseph B. Farrar '65	U.S. Army
Walter Shield, DDS, '65	U.S. Army
F. Willson Craigie '65	U.S. Army
Arthur Lispcomb III '65	U.S. Army
Brandt Everhart '66	U.S. Army
F. Breckinridge Montague '66	U.S. Navy
John D. Drumheller '66	U.S. Navy
John F. Vogel '66	U.S. Army (NGUS)
George S. Kemp III '66	U.S. Army
Edwin G. Ball '66	U.S. Marine Corps
David Dufek '68	U.S. Navy
J. Boyd Spencer '66	U.S. Army
David Mc Laughlin '67	U.S. Army
Gugy A. Irving '67	U.S. Air Force
Thomas Redfern '67	U.S. Army
Jerome P. Brumby '67	U.S. Air Force
William Y. White '68	U.S. Navy
Frank Henson '69	U.S. Marine Corps
James A. Packett '70	U.S. Air Force
Guy Andrews '73	U.S Marine Corps
Braxton Valentine III '73	U.S. Marine Corps
Thomas G. Skinner '74	U.S. Army
John C. Lemmon '75	U.S. Marine Corps

Edward Bentley '77	U.S. Marine Corps
Mark Vakos '82	U.S. Army
Richard G. Hobson '82	U.S. Army
Thomas H. Deane '82	U.S. Army
Matthew Smith '84	U.S. Navy
K. C. Rivera '88	U.S. Army
William Radcliffe '88	U.S. Navy
Jay Councill '90	U.S. Army
John Fleet '90	U.S. Navy
Greg Belkin '91	U.S. Navy
Elvin Cabrera '91	U.S. Army
Shelly Gill '92	U.S. Air Force (ANGUS)
Trip Ellis '92	U.S. Marine Corps
John Newton '93	U.S. Army
Edwin Sherman '97	U.S. Army
Peter Scheu '98	U.S. Navy
Meredith Adkins '00	U.S. Navy
Brad Fertig '00	U.S. Coast Guard
Ashton Crabtree '00	U.S. Navy
Drew Brownson '02	U.S. Air Force
Charles N. Lewis '03	U.S. Army
Brooks Auger '03	U.S. Army
Ned Burgwyn '04	U.S. Coast Guard
L. H. Ginn V '04	U.S. Army
Cody J. Tinsley '05	U.S. Army
Matthew Fluhr '07	U.S. Navy

Faculty/Staff veterans:

Robert M. Yarbrough, Jr.	U.S. Army (AAF)
Randal Brown	U.S. Army (NGUS)
William D. Smith	U.S. Army
Richard J. Bromley	U.S. Army
C. Edwin Cox, Jr.	U.S. Coast Guard
Gerald L. Cooper '53	U.S. Navy
Hatcher C. Williams	U.S. Army
William J. Davies	U.S. Army (AAF)
William Ferrell	U.S. Navy
Robert C. Goodman, Jr.	U.S. Army
Thomas L. Grove, MD	U.S. Army
Henry S. Hackney	U.S. Army (AAF)

Grover C. Jones, Jr.	U.S. Navy
Edward Kearney, MD	U.S. Army (AAF)
Lawrence E. Jensen	U.S. Coast Guard
Albert E. McCue	U.S. Army
Floyd Milby	U.S. Navy
William A. Nunn	U.S. Army
Fredric D. Riley	U.S. Navy
Truman D. Shearer	U.S. Army
William A. Schroeder, Jr.	U.S. Navy
Frank Smart	U.S. Navy
Peter Southmayd	U.S. Marine Corps
James C. Taylor, Jr.	U.S. Navy
William Young	U.S. Navy
R. Christian Willaford	U.S. Navy
Willis Wills	U.S. Coast Guard
Dick Working	U.S. Army (AAF)
William H. Evans III	U.S. Army
Robert A. Shriver	U.S. Navy

APPENDIX B

Personal Awards/Service Medals.
Awarded to Christchurch School Faculty and Alumni

Navy Cross

         Colonel William H. Dabney, USMC
         Captain William D. Young, USN

Distinguished Service Medal

         Vice Admiral John W. Craine, Jr., USN

Silver Star

         Colonel William H. Dabney, USMC
         1st Lieutenant C. Fletcher Flemer III, USA
         Lieutenant Richie N. Henderson, USN
         1st Lieutenant Lewis B. Puller, Jr., USMC
         Captain Sydney A. Vincent, Jr., USA
         Sergeant Joseph B. Farrar, USA

Legion of Merit

         Captain William C. Robards, USN
         Captain Robert A. Shriver, USN
         Captain William A. Schroeder, USN
         Vice Admiral John W. Craine, Jr., USN

Distinguished Flying Cross

         Lt. Colonel David E. Latane, USAF
         Colonel Frederick Anthony, USMC
         Captain William A. Schroeder, USN

Bronze Star Medal

         Colonel Willliam H. Dabney, USMC
         Major L. Winder Lane, USA

1st Lieutnant C. Fletcher Flemer III, USA
Lt. Colonel Cecil W. Page, USA
Captain Nathaniel P. Ward IV, USA
1st Lieutenant George Warren IV, USA
Sergeant Joseph Farrar, USA
T/Sgt Robert H. Mumper, USAAF
Lt. Colonel Raymond R. Goodhart, USA
Colonel William A. Nunn, USA
Captain Cody J. Tinsley, USA
Captain Louis H. Ginn, USA
Major Robert M. Yarbrough, Jr., USA

Navy and Marine Corps Medal[129]

Lieutenant (Junior Grade) Frederick D. Goodwin, Jr., USN

Purple Heart Medal

Captain Thomas S. Marchant, USAAF
Captain Nathaniel P. Ward IV, USA
Lieutenant Richie N. Henderson, USN
Lieutenant Lewis B. Puller, Jr., USMC
Sergeant Joseph Farrar, USA
William "Mick" Bowman, USA
PFC Lewis B. Cardozo, USMC
Captain Sydney A. Vincent, Jr., USA
Lieutenant Hunter Wagener, USA
Radioman Seaman R. H. Langley-Wood, USN

Defense Meritorious Service Medal

Captain Alexander G. Monroe, USN
Lt. Colonel Mark Vakos, USA

Joint Services Commendation Medal

Lt. Colonel Mark Vakos, USA

Joint Services Achievement Medal

Lt. Colonel Mark Vakos, USA
Sergeant Major Thomas H. Deane, USA

Meritorious Service Medal

Vice Admiral John W. Craine, Jr., USN
Captain Alexander G. Monroe, USN

Lt. Colonel Mark Vakos, USA
Sergeant Major Thomas H. Deane, USA

Air Medal

Vice Admiral John W. Craine, Jr., USN
T/Sergeant V. Randolph Chowning, USAAF
1st Lieutenant C. Fletcher Flemer III, USA
Lt. Colonel Fielding Greaves, USA
Lt. Colonel David E. Latane, USAF
Captain Thomas S. Marchant, USAAF
1st Lieutenant George Warren IV, USA
T/Sgt Robert H. Mumper, USAAF
Lt. Colonel Raymond R. Goodhart, USA
Captain William A. Schroeder, USN
1st Lieutenant Herbert S. Osborn, USAAF

Navy Commendation Medal

Vice Admiral John W. Craine, USN
Colonel William H. Dabney, USMC
Captain Alexander G. Monroe, USN
Captain Frederic D. Riley, USN
Captain William C. Robards, USN
Master Chief Jesse L. Hinson, USN

Army Commendation Medal

Lt. Colonel Mark Vakos, USA
Lt. Colonel Raymond Goodhart, USA
Lieutenant Cdr. Roger Garlow, USCG
1st Lieutenant C. Fletcher Flemer III
Captain Ward R. Scull, USA
Sergeant Major Thomas H. Deane, USA
Captain Cody J. Tinsley, USA

Army Achievement Medal

Lt. Colonel Mark Vakos, USA
Captain Louis H. Ginn V, USA
Captain Cody J. Tinsley, USN

Navy Achievement Medal

Vice Admiral John W. Craine, Jr., USN
CDR Breckinridge Montague, USN
Master Chief Jesse L. Hinson, USN

Coast Guard Achievement Medal
>Lt. Commander Roger Garlow, USCG
>Lieutenant Collinson E. P. Burgwyn III, USCG

Coast Guard Commandant's Letter of Commendation with Ribbon
>Lieutenant Collinson E. P. Burgwyn III, USCG

Unit Awards
>Presidential Unit Citation (Navy)
>Navy Unit Commendation (Navy)
>Meritorious Unit Commendation (Navy)

Service and Campaign Ribbons
>American Defense Medal
>China Service Medal
>American Theater of Operations
>Asiatic Pacific Service
>European-North African Service
>Navy Occupation Service
>Army Occupation Service
>National Defense Service Medal
>Vietnam Service Medal
>Armed Forces Expeditionary Medal
>Southwest Asia Service Medal
>Global War on Terror Service Medal

Appendix C

The President of the United States takes pleasure
in presenting the Navy Cross to:

WILLIAM H. DABNEY, COLONEL (then Captain),
U.S. MARINE CORPS

for extraordinary heroism while serving as Commanding Officer of two heavily reinforced rifle companies of the Third Battalion, Twenty-Sixth Marines, THIRD Marine Division (Reinforced), Fleet Marine Force, in connection with operations against the enemy in the Republic of Vietnam from 21 January to 14 April 1968. During the entire period, Colonel Dabney's force stubbornly defended Hill 881S, a regional outpost vital to the defense of the Khe Sanh Combat Base.

Following his bold spoiling attack on 20 January 1968, shattering a much larger North Vietnamese Army (NVA) force deploying to attack Hill 881S, Colonel Dabney's force was surrounded and cut off from all outside ground supply for the entire 77-day Siege of Khe Sanh. Enemy snipers, machine guns, artillery, and 120-millimeter mortars responded to any daylight movement on his position. In spite of deep entrenchments, his total casualties during the siege were close to 100 percent. Helicopters were his only source of re-supply, and each such mission brought down a cauldron of fire on his landing zones. On numerous occasions Colonel Dabney raced into the landing zone under heavy hostile fire to direct debarkation of personnel and to carry wounded Marines to evacuation helicopters.

The extreme difficulty of re-supply resulted in conditions of hardship and deprivation seldom experienced by American forces. Nevertheless, Colonel Dabney's indomitable spirit was truly an inspiration to his troops. He organized his defenses with masterful skill and his preplanned fires shattered every enemy probe on his positions. He also devised an early warning system whereby NVA artillery and rocket firings from the west were immediately reported by lookouts to the Khe Sanh Combat Base, giving exposed personnel a few life-saving seconds to take cover, saving countless lives, and facilitating the targeting of enemy firing positions.

Colonel Dabney repeatedly set an incredible example of calm courage under fire, gallantly exposing himself at the center of every action without concern for his own safety. Colonel Dabney contributed decisively to ultimate victory in the Battle of Khe Sanh, and ranks among the most heroic stands of any American force in history. By his valiant combat leadership, exceptional bravery, and selfless devotion to duty, Colonel Dabney reflected great credit upon himself and upheld the highest traditions of the Marine Corps and the United States Naval Service.

Appendix D

Headmasters of Christchurch School

1921–1924 The Reverend Mr. F. Ernest Warren

1924–1927 Barton Palmer

1927–1934 The Reverend Mr. W. Page Dame

1934–1942 William D. Smith

1942–1943 George L. Barton, Jr.

1943–1946 The Reverend Mr. Janney Hutton

1946–1949 James Radcliffe

1949–1957 Branch Spalding

1957–1971 Robert M. Yarbrough, Jr.

1971–1974 The Reverend Dr. William P. Scheel

1974–1984 Louis W. Randall

1983–1984 Benjamin J. Boneventura

1984–1994 The Reverend Mr. Robert S. Phipps

1994–1995 C. Jackson Blair

1995–2000 David H. Charlton

2000–Present John E. Byers

ENDNOTES

1   Vice Admiral John W. Craine, Jr., '64, USN, entered the Navy through the Aviation Officer Candidate Program and served in increasingly responsible assignments. He was commanding officer of Fighter Squadron Eighty-Four, nicknamed *The Jolly Rogers* and later commanded the Naval Air Station Oceana. He retired as a Vice Admiral and assumed duty as president of the State University of New York, Maritime College at Fort Schuyler, Throggs Neck, the Bronx, New York.

2   The institutions represented by these men are: Choate Rosemary Hall, Phillips Academy Andover, St. George's School, Episcopal High School, St. Albans School and Darrow School.

3   William Styron, "Christchurch," an address delivered by William Styron at Christchurch School (Briarpatch Press: Davidson, N.C.), May 28, 1975, p. 2.

4   Roy Jenkins, *Churchill, A Biography* (Penguin Putnam: New York), 2001, p. 621.

5   Winston S. Churchill, *The Second World War, Their Finest Hour* (Boston: Houghton Mifflin Co., 1949), p. 401. In a cable to President Franklin Roosevelt, Churchill felt "bound to put the gravity and urgency of the position before you."

6   See Air University, Maxwell-Gunter AFB, "Gathering of Eagles site," Biography of Ensign (later Captain) Leonard B. "Tuck" Smith, USN. See also KBismarck.com, Report of the Scouting and Search for Bismarck by Ensign Smith, Intelligence Report 1066 dated June 9, 1941. Aircraft overflew neutral Irish territory to reach patrol stations in the Atlantic.

7   See Ltr (S/DECL), Commander Task Group 3.6 to Chief of Naval Operations, "German Motorship *Odenwald* disguised as SS *Willmoto* United States Registry-Seizure of," November 12, 1941. The German crew had attempted to scuttle the ship and thus under maritime law the prize crew were salvors and each later received $3,000.

8   USS *Spearfish* came to Corregidor on May 3, 1942, three days before

it fell. Among those evacuated was Lieutenant Ann Bernatitus (NC) USN, one of the Navy nurses who had cared for patients in the Malinta Tunnel and was decorated with the Legion of Merit.

9   Freeland Mason '41 e-mail message to author May 30, 2011; William Ray Winder '42 letter to Deane H. Hundley, Director of Alumni Affairs, Christchurch School, n.d.

10 His brother, Forrest Byrd Holloway '42 served in the 11th Airborne Division of the United States Army in the Pacific. He died in 2007 and is buried beside his brother at Flintshire Farm, Caroline County, Virginia.

11 The War Diary of the 535th Heavy Bombardment Squadron notes that there was cloud cover from the Hook of Holland to the target and that after dropping its bombs, In Like Errol lost altitude rapidly because two engines were lost.

12 Ken Stone, ed., Triumphant We Fly, A 381st Bomb Group Anthology, privately printed 1985, p. 153.

13 IOI, Missing Air Crew Report #13542/Case 3977, 30 March 1945. The flight originated in Ridgewell, United Kingdom, and the target was Bremen, Germany. The aircraft was shot down at about 2:09 PM as it completed its bombing run over Bremen and turned to return to England.

14 Christ Episcopal Church, the institution for which the school is named, "Christ Church," and its name is so spelled. In the period 1958–1960, there were two school buses. The marking of one was "Christchurch," and the other "Christ Church."

15 IOI, data card of The Navy Department's Board of Decorations and Medals in the case of Lt. Richie Henderson, USN. The Awards Board met on April 5, 1944, and recommended award of the Silver Star medal to Lt. Henderson. The medal, the card notes, was mailed to his next of kin on May 5, 1944.

16 James Good Brown, Chaplain of the 381st Heavy Bombardment Group, The Mighty Men of the 381st: Heroes All, privately published, 1985. The flyleaf is inscribed to his friend S/Sergeant Charles (Chuck) Majors, USAAF, who saved his life. It reads, "Chuck, I can never thank you enough for your help when my chute opened and you had the guts to help me into another chute. God was with us on March 30th, 1945."

17 See oral history of Joseph B. Farrar '65 conducted by Alexander G. Monroe, Class of 1960, dated August 27, 2005, an abstract of which is held by M. Huntley Galleher, Associate Director of Development, Christchurch School.

18 Wyllie joined the American Field Service in October 1941 and was sent to the Middle East as an ambulance driver. He served in Syria and with the British Eighth Army until November 1942, when he was repatriated and ultimately joined the U.S. Army Air Force. After the war, he became librarian of the University of Virginia.

19 The letter from Commander Submarine Force Pacific Fleet recommending him for the Navy Cross speaks of Lieutenant Richie Henderson's "extraordinary heroism in the line of duty ... in a position of great responsibility ... in enemy patrolled waters ... in penetrating dangerous enemy waters . . . where he contributed to the known destruction of one important enemy vessel ..." See also Commanding Officer Naval Air Station Norfolk letter NAS/P15:95-By-pd of April 6, 1944. The letter praises Lieutenant (Junior Grade) Frederick D. Goodwin, Jr., '38, USN, for "presence of mind and fearless action" on January 14, 1944, which resulted in rescuing another naval aviator from a burning aircraft just before its fuel tank exploded. The Navy and Marine Corps Medal was conferred on July 7, 1944, at Naval Air Station Norfolk.

20 IOI, Report of Separation in the case of 1st Lt. Thomas S. Marchant, AC, USA, dated January 27, 1946.

21 See again the earlier reference to S/Sgt. Bob Mumper's experience with spoiled food. Clearly they missed the gustatory treats regularly produced by Christchurch chef Joseph C. Cameron, denoted "an almost global legend" by William Styron '42. The reference to the rat is from an e-mail communication of September 28, 2010, from Thomas S. Marchant, Jr., to the author.

22 IOI, "Encounter Report-Romilly," w/att'd Interrogation Documents and Mission Loading Lists, December 20, 1942.

23 Seventy-six prisoners escaped on March 25, 1944, and seventy-three were rapidly apprehended. On the direct order of Hitler, fifty were summarily executed by the SS. News of the atrocity was shared with the House of Commons by Foreign Minister Anthony Eden in May 1944.

24 Thomas S. Marchant, Jr., e-mail message to the author, September 28, 2010.

25 This evaluation of Richie Henderson is contained in a squib adjacent to his photograph in the 1940 "Lucky Bag," the yearbook of the United States Naval Academy at Annapolis.

26 Wakkani later became a U.S. Air Force Station, a Cold War "listening post." It was also a support base for the U.S. Navy and ships involved in reconnaissance operations such as the net layer USS *Etlah* (AN-

79). The executive officer, Lieutenant (Junior Grade) Thomas C. Barker, USN, later Dean of the School of Allied Health Professions at the Medical College of Virginia, recalled that though the ship's company was aware of the loss of the USS *Wahoo* (SS-238), they never found any trace of it in their work, which included lowering nets in the strait's waters.

27   Commanding Officer of the USS *Sawfish* (SS-276) was Lieutenant Commander Eugene T. Sands, USN, the grandfather of Sergeant Major Thomas H. Deane '82, USA.

28   David Bercurson and Holger Herwig, *One Christmas in Washington* (New York: Overlook Press, 2005), p. 126-28. Prime Minister Winston Churchill had feared that the attack on Pearl Harbor would make President Franklin Roosevelt abandon his "Europe first" strategy for dealing with the Axis powers.

29   Coincidentally, Ensign Alexander Monroe   '60, USN, served as gunnery officer and underway officer of the deck on the *Aucilla* twenty-one years later. His commanding officer was Captain Tazewell Shepard, Jr., USN, former naval aide to President John F. Kennedy. Captain Shepard went on to command USS *Princeton* (LPH-5), on which John Drumheller '66, brother of F. Davis Drumheller '60, served.

30   Memo, Medical Officer, USS *Belknap* (APD-34) to Bureau of Medicine and Surgery, Navy Department, Washington, D.C., "Casualty Reports," January 17, 1945. The initial report, submitted by Lieutenant E. L. Coffin (MC) USNR, notes 14 KIA, 4 MIA and 55 WIA.

31   IOI, History of USS *Belknap* (APD-34), Ships' History Division, Navy Department, January 7, 1953. See also letter of Captain Benjamin T. Brooks, USN (Ret.), formerly commanding officer of USS *Belknap* (APD-34) to Director of the Navy Museum, May 23, 1985. Captain Brooks was commanding officer of USS *Belknap* (APD-34) until September 1944 and then commanding officer of USS *Begor* (APD-127).

32   Nineteen soldiers from the small town of Bedford, Virginia, were killed at Omaha Beach and three additional soldiers were lost in subsequent operations in Normandy. The loss was proportionately greater than any sustained by any other American community in the war.

33   Center for Military History (CMH), U.S. Army, CMH Publication 100-13, 21 August 1946, p. 118; See also World War Two Memorial homepage, which notes that his place of burial is the American

Cemetery at Normandy, Plot C, Row 20, grave 32.

34   In part, Hitler and his subordinates used the secret "Night and Fog" (Nacht und Nebel) Decree to remove those suspected of complicity in the plot from their homes in the dead of night. This terrifying technique, which involved abruptly entering the victim's home unexpectedly, was brought into being on December 7, 1941, and used throughout occupied Europe and then in Germany itself as the war became more desperate.

35   "Americans Stall German Drive in Luxembourg," *Richmond Times-Dispatch*, December 25, 1944; Ladislas Farago, *Patton, Ordeal and Triumph* (New York: Astor-Honor, Inc. 1964), p. 690.

36   One individual who was, according to his son-in-law, very reluctant to speak of his achievements was Herbert S. Osborn,'39, who served as navigator of a B-24 in the attacks on Romanian oil fields and refineries at Ploesti, the source of sixty percent of Germany's crude oil. Osborn received the Air Medal for his service in these exceedingly dangerous missions.

37   Jim Davenport died on April 26, 2012, and his May 4, 2012, obituary in the Norfolk *Virginian-Pilot* said, among other things, that he believed in contributing to the well-being of the community in which he lived.

38   IOI, Discussion between the author and Robert C. Goodman, Jr., former academic dean of Christchurch School of October 23, 2010.

39   Whittaker Chambers, *Witness* (New York: Random House, 1952), p. 420.

40   Alger Hiss was an honors graduate of Johns Hopkins University and Harvard Law School. He served as law clerk to Oliver Wendell Holmes, Jr. The so-called "Hiss case" brought Richard M. Nixon to national attention.

41   Wilson D. Miscamble, *From Roosevelt to Truman, Potsdam, Hiroshima and the Cold War* (Cambridge, England and New York: Cambridge University Press, 2007), Preface.

42   The imposition of quarantine was announced in the evening of October 22, 1962. It was brought into being by the President's signing Proclamation 3504, dealing with the interdiction of offensive weapons bound for Cuba on October 23, 1962.

43   The Naval History and Heritage Command's homepage notes that USS *Corry* (DDR-817) was awarded the Armed Forces Expeditionary Medal for service in interdiction operations for the periods October 24–November 12 and November 18–21, 1962. The award data is also shown in the Navy Personnel Command's web site, commonly known

as NDAWS: https://awards.navy.mil/awards/webbas01.

44 IOI, RD2 James Shaftic, "History of USS *Corry* (DD-817) February 1961–August 1963," www.USS-Corry-dd817.org; see also deck logbook, USS *Corry* (DDR-817), July-August, 1963.

45 Lieutenant Colonel Gugy A. Irving III '67, USAF, describes in his oral history the turbulence at Hobart College in Upstate New York where the Air Force ROTC building was firebombed by dissidents.

46 Colonel Dabney's account of those times is given in a videotaped oral history to be found at virtual usmcmuseum.com of the Marine Corps Museum and Heritage Center at Quantico, Virginia.

47 1ˢᵗ Lieutenant Puller's father was Lieutenant General Lewis B. Puller, USMC (1898–1971). He earned five Navy Crosses, one Distinguished Service Cross, the Silver Star and the Legion of Merit. He retired in 1955 as Commanding General of the Second Marine Division at Camp Lejeune, North Carolina.

48 The clash in views is explained fully in *Fortunate Son, Healing of a Vietnam Vet*, Grove Press, 1991, p. 268.

49 Letter, Commanding Officer, 3ʳᵈ Reconnaissance Battalion to Commandant of the Marine Corps (Code AO3D), "Command Chronology for 1 December 1968–31 December 1968," January 9, 1969.

50 As of 2013, HSC Two is homeported at Naval Base Norfolk, and its detachment is deployed to the Fifth Fleet at Manama, Bahrain and is known as "the Desert Ducks."

51 The abbreviation for the base at Guantanamo Bay, Cuba, which is used on cargo containers and aircraft passenger manifests and the like, is GTMO. Over the years it has become known as Gitmo, in part for ease of pronunciation.

52 Myra McPherson, "McNamara's 'other' crimes: the stories you haven't heard—Robert S. McNamara," Washington Monthly, June 1995, p. 28.

53 U.S. Congress. House Committee on the Armed Forces, Report by the Special Subcommittee on Disciplinary Problems in the U.S. Navy, 92d, House Armed Services Committee, 92-81, 1973. For further discussion of this episode see *Troubled Water—Race, Mutiny and Bravery on the USS Kitty Hawk*, Gregory A. Freeman (Palgrave-McMillan, a division of St. Martin's Press, 2009).

54 Then Captain John W. Craine, Jr., '64, USN, served under Admiral Boorda as air operations officer for Cruiser Destroyer Group Eight in Norfolk, Virginia, and later the special assistant for Flag Matters to the Chief of Naval Personnel, also known as "flag officer detailer," for

Vice Admiral Boorda.

55 The General Assembly of the United Nations adopted by 108–9 Resolution 387 that condemned the invasion, which "constitutes a flagrant violation of international law ..." President Reagan observed that the lopsided nature of the General Assembly vote "didn't upset his breakfast at all."

56 The Prime Minister observed that this might present difficulties in the government's consideration of permitting the locating of American cruise missiles in the United Kingdom.

57 Susan Bennett, "House Demands Reagan Explain Persian Gulf Strategy," *The Philadelphia Inquirer*, June 3, 1987.

58 During the operation, General Colin Powell, Chairman of the Joint Chiefs of Staff, observed in a press conference that Manuel Noriega didn't demonstrate the characteristics of endurance that would make him a good fugitive.

59 The operations that might be required were earlier known as Blue Spoon and Bushmaster and renamed. The commander on the ground was General Maxwell R. Thurman, USA (1931–1995), Commander of the United States Southern Command.

60 Admiral Leon A. Edney, USN, then commander-in-chief of the United States Atlantic Command at Norfolk, Virginia, used this phrase in a message to General Colin L. Powell, USA, to describe the situation in Haiti and the Windward Passage after the fall of Jean Bertrand Aristide, president of Haiti.

61 See oral history of Captain Stephen Koehler, USN, former Commanding Officer USS *Bataan* (LHD-5), and Commander Ryan McCormick, USN, dated February 25, 2010. The ship had just finished a deployment to the Mediterranean and was scheduled to enter the shipyard in February 2010. The ship was in a safety stand-down and had been "cold iron" for thirty-six days and was made ready for sea in less than forty-eight hours.

62 William Styron, *Lie Down in Darkness* (New York: Bobbs-Merrill, 1951), p. 235.

63 James L. W. West III, *William Styron, A Life* (New York: Random House, 1998), p. 5.

64 Commander (now Admiral) James G. Stavridis, USN, "A Perfect Form One," U.S. Naval Institute Proceedings, October 1995, p. 45-7.

65 In a letter to Mr. Yarbrough, dated October 9, 2006, William G. Broaddus '61, a former attorney general of Virginia, praised the headmaster as a "constant" in his life and explicitly compared him to the Rappahannock River: "You have rolled on, sometimes quietly, but

always strong, always there," in his life, as he had been in the lives of countless others.

66 Colonel Dabney's gallantry as a Marine Corps captain at Hill 881 S in Vietnam was recognized belatedly by award of the Navy Cross, the second highest award for bravery, prior to his death on February 15, 2012, in Lexington, Virginia.

67 Lewis B. Puller, Jr., *Fortunate Son*, (New York: Bantam Books, 1993) p. 308.

68 The school admitted girls as boarders in the fall of 2012.

69 See oral history of Robert A. McMillan '61 conducted by Alexander G. Monroe '60 at Christchurch School, dated June 11, 2011, a copy of which is held by M. Huntley Galleher, Associate Director of Development, Christchurch School.

70 See oral history of H. Murrell McLeod '58, conducted by Alexander G. Monroe '60, dated January 2, 2006, an abstract of which is held by M. Huntley Galleher, Associate Director of Development, Christchurch School.

71 See again oral history of Murrell McLeod '58.

72 See again oral history of Robert A. McMillan '61.

73 See oral history of Somerville Parker conducted by Alexander G. Monroe '60, dated August 6, 2005, an abstract of which is held by M. Huntley Galleher, Associate Director of Development, Christchurch School.

74 See oral history of C. Nelson "Nellie" Williams IV '61 conducted by Alexander G. Monroe '60, dated August 23, 2005, an abstract of which is held by M. Huntley Galleher, Associate Director of Development, Christchurch School.

75 J. Everette "Ebo" Fauber '56 remembers the shock of seeing cubicles for the first time. He said he thought "he was in a stable, with horse stalls." Actually, they were somewhat more commodious and had more privacy than the junior officer bunkrooms on an aircraft carrier, frequently known as "boys' town" or "ensign lockers" on a destroyer.

76 See oral history of Meredith D. Adkins '00 conducted by Alexander G. Monroe '60, dated January, 2012, abstract of which is held by M. Huntley Galleher, Associate Director of Development, Christchurch School.

77 This gentleman is the father of Herbert Scott Osborn '39, who served in the U.S. Army Air Force as a navigator in the landmark raids on Romanian oil refineries at Ploesti and in so doing earned the Air Medal.

78 Colgan Hobson Bryan, Sr., left Christchurch and assumed teaching

duties at the University of Alabama in aerospace engineering and was at the university for sixty-three years. He died on June 4, 2006.

79 By coincidence, he was commissioned in June 1956, eight years before Alexander G. "Sandy" Monroe. He served in the same ship as a commissioned officer on which Sandy served in July–August 1963 as an NROTC midshipman.

80 James Ratcliff was the seventh headmaster of Christchurch School.

81 During the tenure of Secretary of Defense Donald Rumsfeld, the title was changed to "U.S. Navy Reserve," and personnel are designated "USN" after their names, rather than "USNR." This change was the result of specific language in the National Defense Appropriation Act of 2005. It is related to the fact that since the terrorist attacks of September 11, 2001, armed forces reserve personnel have been increasingly used in operational areas and their performance is indistinguishable from those members of the regular establishment.

82 Roger Alexander Holladay '53

83 Edward H. Littlefield '52

84 USS *Northampton* (CC-1) was one of two ships that served as National Emergency Command Post Afloat (NECPA), to which the president of the United States might be evacuated in the event of nuclear attack or other catastrophic national emergency. It operated off the Atlantic Coast in range of Tropospheric Scatter Communications Facilities. It was in essence an alternate White House with special berthing facilities for high government officials and was staffed by members of all the armed forces. Its voice radio call sign was "Sea Ruler."

85 Captain Cutter, as a midshipman at Annapolis, won the 1935 Army-Navy football game with a field goal in the last three minutes of the game. He earned four Navy Crosses for heroism as commanding officer of USS *Seahorse* (SS-304). Memorabilia from the submarine, as well as a tail rotor from an H-60 helicopter in Helicopter Sea Control Squadron One, nicknamed "the Seahorses," are on display in the basement of Scott-Taylor Hall.

86 Ocean Station duty could be monotonous or exciting. In terms usually applied to naval aviation, it is "hours of boredom punctuated by minutes of stark terror." Cutters assigned to such duty played a role in weather forecasting, and there were noteworthy SAR cases. One that garnered national attention was the rescue, without injury or fatality of the aircrew and passengers, of a Pan American Airways Stratocruiser that was flying from Honolulu to San Francisco. The rescue of Flight 6 and the souls on board by CGC *Ponchartrain* (WHEC-70), on Ocean Station November is a milestone in Coast Guard history that

antedates the January 2009 ditching in the Hudson River of U.S. Airways Flight 1549.

87 Branch Spalding was the eighth Headmaster of Christchurch School.

88 USS *Spiegel Grove* (LSD-32), a Dock Landing Ship of the Atlantic Fleet, was commissioned in 1954 and was named for Spiegel Grove, an estate near Fremont, Ohio, that was the home of Rutherford B. Hayes, nineteenth president of the United States. After a long and distinguished career, the ship was decommissioned in 1989 and moored in the James River Reserve Fleet, also known as the Ghost Fleet, near Fort Eustis, Virginia, until 2002 when she was sunk off Dixie Key, Florida, to serve as an artificial reef in the National Marine Sanctuary.

89 The first two commissioned ranks are ensign and lieutenant (junior grade). There is no seniority among ensigns, and even though lieutenants (junior grade) have seniority based on lineal numbers, they are novices and generally so regarded.

90 An officer of the deck underway may be qualified for task force operations or independent operations. The latter qualification is not as difficult to attain, since the OOD is not operating with other ships in close concentrations. It is unusual for an officer who is in an embarked unit such as a Beachmaster Unit or a Tactical Air Control Squadron to be "qualified underway," also known as "top watch standers." LTJG McMillan was an exceptionally talented officer to be able to do this. Officers in embarked units such as Beachmasters or Tactical Air Control Squadrons were frequently put on the watch bill to ease the load on ship's company officers.

91 USS *Spiegel Grove* (LSD-32) was much more difficult to maneuver and handle than a destroyer because it had a greater draft and higher freeboard that could be affected by the wind and weather, and such ships were often seen as a prelude to increased responsibility and rank. In fact, some were commanded by naval aviators. Most were commanded by captains, whose next rank, if selected for promotion, would be rear admiral. An individual in the Navy trying to reach the next rate as an enlisted person or next rank as an officer is said to be "striking for" it.

92 While in this "blackshoe" (Surface Navy) organization on the waterfront in Norfolk, Virginia, he worked for Rear Admiral Jeremy M. Boorda, USN, who later became Chief of Naval Personnel and Chief of Naval Operations.

93 This assignment was complicated by the fact that President Clinton decided that Cubans no longer qualified for automatic admission to

the United States as political asylees, fleeing a hostile Communist country.

94 John Craine provides an amusing vignette about how Mr. Yarbrough, who had a beaklike nose, formerly known as "Mr. A." (to distinguish him from Mr. E. R. M. Yerburgh, whose name was pronounced the same way), acquired the nickname "the Hawk." According to John, he wore a dark black raincoat around his shoulders when he strode from the senior vocabulary class in the "white house," which burned to the ground some years later. The wind that came off the river caught the coats sleeves and they flapped about. He resembled a hawk, or as Bob put it to generations of students, "a diurnal bird of prey."

95 His gallantry in action was recognized by award of the Silver Star and the Bronze Star (twice awarded). The Special Operations Group (SOG) performed highly sensitive, still classified, duties in the Republic of Vietnam and contiguous nations.

96 "Guinea men" are watermen who earn their living by oystering and crabbing in a remote section of eastern Gloucester County, Virginia, known as Guinea. They are self reliant, hardy individuals who speak a dialect not unlike that of the residents of Tangier Island in the Chesapeake Bay. From time to time, they trespassed on the school's property and on one occasion, of which Joe Farrar speaks, were chased from the premises by then-assistant headmaster, the late Hebert G. Wyatt and "Jungle."

97 This episode is known in Christchurch lore as the tale of the "Unlucky 13," and it has been reported that one of the individuals is now an Episcopal priest in Wyoming.

98 "Black" operations are clandestine in nature, sometimes illegal operations that may be carried on by private companies or governmental entities. There is a negative connotation to such activities, and they are non attributable to the governmental entity executing them. In the past, it has been disclosed that they have been carried out by such organizations as the Federal Bureau of Investigation and the Central Intelligence Agency, as well as military organizations.

99 Captain Frederic Riley had served in USS *Gunnel* (SS-253), a submarine commanded by Senator John McCain's father, and later commanded USS *Monrovia* (APA-31), an attack transport.

100 His older brother is Commander Robert L. Montague III '52, USN.

101 This meant that when he was commissioned, Ensign Montague was paid as an ensign with two years longevity, which meant he would be paid at a considerably higher rate than other newly commissioned ensigns.

102 The records of Task Force 115 show that SS *Green Bay* was sunk by enemy swimmers on August 17, 1972, at Qui Nhon, RVN.

103 One such contemporary is 1st Lt. Lewis B. Puller '63, USMC, who was grievously wounded in Vietnam.

104 The "white house" was the original building of the school. It burned to the ground during the headmastership of Louis Randall.

105 The acronym WAVE stands for Women Accepted for Volunteer Enlisted Service in the U.S. Navy.

106 Sergeant Joseph B. Farrar, U.S. Army, served as a medic in Vietnam. He was wounded once, and his courage was recognized by award of the Silver and 2 Bronze Stars.

107 David Charlton, after a period as acting headmaster, became the 15th headmaster of Christchurch School.

108 The United States Joint Forces Command is the successor to the United States Atlantic Command, a chiefly maritime command established at Norfolk, Virginia, in 1947. It comprises members of all the armed forces. The Commander is dual hatted and serves concurrently as Commander Allied Forces Transformation, formerly known as the Supreme Allied Command Atlantic (SACLANT), the North Atlantic Treaty Organization entity. From 1992 until 2006, Captain Alexander G. Monroe, USN, was assigned to the Office of the Command Historian at U.S. Joint Forces Command.

109 Southern European Task Force, United States Army Forces, Europe.

110 Sergeant Joseph Farrar, U.S. Army.

111 Vice Admiral John W. Craine, Jr., U.S. Navy.

112 Lieutenant Colonel David L. Henderson, U.S. Army.

113 Captain Alexander G. Monroe, U.S. Navy.

114 The June 22, 1970 issue of *TIME* magazine contains an article about "Tommy the Traveler," reported to be an undercover FBI (Federal Bureau of Investigation) who went to various campuses in Upstate New York in an effort to encourage dissident elements to participate in disruptive activities and was involved in firebombing Sherrill Hall, jointly used as a dormitory and Air Force ROTC offices.

115 One of the more charming stories in Christchurch lore refers to the observation made by J. Everette "Ebo" Fauber '57, when he saw a cubicle for the first time. "Ebo" said he thought he was in a stable looking at stalls.

116 Mr. Yarbrough often spoke of the course and opined, "A word a day keeps the college boards at bay." The practice is strong in the memories of those of the Yarbrough era.

117 "Hooah" is a generally used response or cheer used by U.S. Army

personnel. It is thought to mean "yes," "yes sir," or "that's great." One explanation of the meaning holds that it is derived from the word "hurrah." Another explanation is that it is of British origin, and is the phonetic spelling of the word HUA meaning "heard, understood and acknowledged." That explanation holds that the expression was used by British military forces in Afghanistan.

118 United States Southern Command, under the ground command of General Maxwell R. Thurman, USA.

119 This abbreviation denotes the High Mobility Multipurpose Wheeled Vehicle, also known as the "Humvee."

120 See Navy.mil, IOI, "*Bataan* assisting in Hurricane Katrina Relief Efforts," NNSO050832-02, USS *Bataan* (LHD-5), Public Affairs Office, August 31, 2005. The ship was returning to Norfolk from Exercise PANAMEX 2005 and was diverted to the Gulf Coast, where it remained for nineteen days providing humanitarian assistance.

121 The ship was returning helicopters to Naval Station Ingleside, Texas.

122 The ship was tasked for operations on August 30, 2005. By the same day at 5:00 P.M., MH60s Seahawks from Helicopter Logistic Squadron Twenty Eight were deployed ashore to render assistance, and by 6:00 P.M. the same day, MH53 Sea Stallions from Helicopter Mine Countermeasures Squadron 15 (HM15) based at Naval Air Station Corpus Christi and deployed to the ship were likewise en route ashore.

123 USS *Bataan* (LHD-5) is a major heavy lift amphibious ship designed to support significant operations, and as such it has a staff capable of fulfilling medical or dental needs of the ship's company or embarked Marines.

124 During this period the ship had two "fly-away" medical teams embarked, and they provided medical care ashore.

125 Admiral Thad W. Allen, USCG was placed in overall command of Hurricane Katrina relief operations. He succeeded Michael D. Brown, Director of the Federal Emergency Management Agency (FEMA), whose efforts were ineffectual.

126 Lieutenant General Russel L. Honore, USA, who was commanding general of the First United States Army, was in charge of Joint Task Force Katrina, that entity that coordinated military relief operations in the New Orleans/Gulf Coast area.

127 IOI, "NH Jacksonville Medical Team Deploy to Aid Hurricane Victims," NNS050902-06, Loren Barnes, Public Affairs Office, September 2, 2005.

128 Since he did the oral history, Lieutenant Burgwyn has been promoted

from Lieutenant (Junior Grade) to Lieutenant and has been assigned as aide to the commander of the First Coast Guard District.

129 The Navy and Marine Corps Medal is different from the Navy and Marine Corps Commendation Medal. It is awarded for heroism that does not necessarily entail action against an armed enemy but rather lifesaving. For example, Lieutenant John F. Kennedy was awarded the medal for his performance in rescuing crewmen after the sinking of the PT-109.

BIBLIOGRAPHY

Books

Churchill, Winston S., *Their Finest Hour*, New York, Houghton Mifflin Co., 1949.

Burcurson, David and Holger Herwig, *One Christmas in Washington*, Overlook Press, 2005.

Farago, Ladislas, *Patton: Ordeal and Triumph*, Astor-Honor, Incorporated, New York, 1964.

Manchester, William and Reid, Paul, *The Last Lion, Winston Spencer Churchill Defender of the Realm*, Little, Brown and Company, New York, 2012.

Jenkins, Roy, *Churchill: A Biography*, A Plume Book, 2001.

Styron, William C., *Lie Down in Darkness*, New York, Vintage International Books, 1992.

West, James L. W. III, *William Styron, A Life*, New York, Random House, 1998.

Articles and Official Reports

Anonymous, "Report of Death in the case of Major Charles L. Darbie, INF, USA," War Department, The Adjutant General's Office, Washington, February 17, 1945.

Anonymous, "Missing Air Crew Report, Aircraft Serial Number 42-102590," Nicknamed In Like Errol, Case 3997, War Department, Headquarters Army Air Forces, Washington.

Anonymous, "The Lucky Bag," U.S. Naval Academy Yearbook, June 1940, Annapolis, Maryland.

Anonymous, "Mission Loading List in the case of U.S. Army aircraft Serial number 41-24495," Homepage of the 306th Heavy Bombardment Group.

Anonymous, "Officer Biography in the case of Commander Miles A. Libbey, USN, U.S. Navy," Biographies Branch (OI450), Washington, September 22, 1953.

Anonymous, "Officer Biography in the case of Commander Frederic D. Riley, USN, U.S. Navy," Biographies Branch (OI450), Washington, February 1, 1956.

Anonymous, "Officer Biography in the case of Captain William C. F. Robards, USN," U.S. Navy Biographies Branch (OI450), Washington, August 1, 1956.

Anonymous, "Transcript of Service in the case of Lieutenant Richie Neale Henderson, U.S. Navy, Active, Deceased," File Number 085127, Bureau of Naval Personnel (Pers 5323a-lk), Washington, February 8, 1946.

Commander James G. Stavridis, USN, "A Perfect Form One," U.S. Naval Institute Proceedings, October 1995.

Corporal Ray Ingham, USAAF, "War diary of the 535th Heavy Bombardment Squadron, 381st Heavy Bombardment Group," March 1945.

Oral History Interviews, Written Accounts, Letters, Papers

Anonymous, academic record card of Sydney Archibald Vincent, Jr., Class of 1940, Virginia Military Institute, June 12, 1940.

Anonymous, data card for re-issues of the VMI Register for Former Cadets in the case of Captain Sydney Archibald Vincent, Jr., USA, May 16, 1945.

Anonymous, index card of the Secretary of the Navy's Board for Decorations and Medals in the case of Lieutenant (Junior Grade) Frederick Dean Goodwin, Jr., USN.

Anonymous, index card of the Secretary of the Navy's Board for Decorations and Medals in the case of Lieutenant Richie N. Henderson, USN, USS Wahoo (SS-238).

Broaddus, William G., letter to Robert M. Yarbrough, Jr., Ninth Headmaster of Christchurch School, October 9, 2006.

Chandler, Captain Theodore E., USN, Commander Task Group 3.6. Letter to Chief of Naval Operations, "German Motorship Odenwald Disguised as SS Willmoto, United States Registry-Seizure of, November 12, 1941.

Brown, Chaplain James Good, USAAF, The Mighty Men of the 381st: Heroes All, n.d.

Julian, Colonel Gregory S., USA, with attachment of Admiral James G. Stravridis, USN, e-mail communication to Alexander G. Monroe, February 2, 2012.

Lupia, Commander Archy L., USN, Deck Log Book, USS Corry (DDR-817), July 15, 1963.

Majors, Sergeant Charles L., USAAF, letter to Nancy Mumper, April 21, 1998.

IN SERVICE TO THEIR COUNTRY

Marchant, Thomas S., Jr., e-mail communication to Alexander G. Monroe, September 28, 2010.

Mason, T. Freeland, e-mail communication to Alexander G. Monroe, May 30, 2011.

Mumper, Nancy, letter to Alexander G. Monroe, November 27, 2010.

Shaftic, James L., Radarman, Second Class, USN, History of USS *Corry* (DDR-817), USS *Corry* Association Homepage.

Smith, William D., Headmaster of Christchurch School, Certificate of Recommendation for Admission to Virginia Military Institute in the case of Sydney A. Vincent, Jr., Class of 1936.

Stanik, Joseph D., *Swift and Effective Retribution: The U.S. Sixth Fleet and the Confrontation with Qaddafi*, (Naval Historical Center), Washington, 1996.

Stone, Ken, *Triumphant We Fly, A 381ˢᵗ Bomb Group Anthology*, 1943-45, n.d.

Styron, Rose, letter to Alexander G. Monroe, February 23, 2012.

Styron, William C., "Christchurch," commencement address, May 28, 1975.

Utz, Curtis, *Cordon of Steel: The U.S. Navy and the Cuban Missile Crisis*, (Naval Historical Center), Washington, 1993.

Winder, William Ray, e-mail communication to Alexander G. Monroe, March 28, 2011.

Winder, William Ray, copy of letter to Deane H. Hundley, Director of Alumni Affairs, Christchurch School, n.d.

Winder, William Ray, copy of letter to children of William Fife Boone Bowman, n.d.

Newspapers

New York Times
Richmond News Leader
Richmond Times-Dispatch
Vicksburg Post

Index

Gonzales, Eduardo, 25

Goodhart, Raymond R., 31

Goodman, Robert C., Jr., xvii, 23–24, 88

Goodwin, Richard, 120

"Great Grey Ghost of the Virginia Coast". *See* National Emergency Command Post Afloat (NECPA)

Greatest Generation, 8

Gregory, Edward M. "Pope" (Reverend), 52, 123

Gregory, Willis M., 31

Grieves, Jennifer, 50, 131

Grove, Thomas L., MD, 7–8, 33

GTMO. *See* Guantanamo Bay, Cuba (Naval Base)

Guantanamo Bay, Cuba (Naval Base), 25, 34, 40–41, 98

Gulf of Tonkin Resolution, 28

H

Harwood, Woodford, 9

Helicopter Combat Support Squadron Two, 33

Helicopter Sea Combat Support Squadron 2 (HSC2), 33

Henderson, Richie N., 6–7, 13–14, 16, 22, 46, 48, 118

HIMJS *Ataka*, 36

Hinson, Jesse L., 31, 72–75

Hiss, Alger, 24

HMM364. *See* Marine Medium Helicopter Squadron 364 (HMM364)

Holladay, Clem, 68

Holloway, Forrest Byrd, 4

Holloway, Robert G., 6

Honore, Russel L., 129

Hopewell, John S., 31, 46, 49

Horton, Malcus, 4

Hoy, Emmet, Jr. (Reverend), xvii, 48, 72–73

Humanitarian Assistance (HA), 40

Humanitarian Missions, Military, 34, 40–41

Hussein, Saddam, 42–44, 124

I

In Like Errol, 4–5, 7–8

Intercontinental Ballistic Missiles (ICBMs), 25–26

Irving, Gugy A., 43, 53–54, 116, 120–122

J

Jean Bart, 4

Jefferson, Garland, 32

Jihad, 43

Johnson, Lyndon B., 34

Joint Task Force Middle East, 39, 41, 117

Jones, Bill, 12, 48

Jones, Grover C., Jr., xvii, 72, 90, 93, 95, 106, 136

K

Karbala Provincial Reconstruction Team, 43

Karr, Harry E., 9

Katrina, Hurricane, 128

Kearney, Edward L., MD, 3, 17, 21, 33, 58

Kelley, Paul X., 103

Kennedy, John F., xix, 25–27, 46

Kennedy, Granville Marvin, 14

Kristallnacht, 1

L

Langley-Wood, Robertson "Doc", 17, 21, 58

Lend Lease Act, 2

Libbey, Miles A., Jr., 3–4, 46

Littlefield, Ward, 68

M

MAAG. *See* Military Assistance Advisory Group (MAAG)

MacArthur, Douglas, 3

MACV. *See* Military Assistance Advisory Command Vietnam (MACV)

Majors, Chuck, 4–5, 7–8

Marchant, Thomas A., 9, 11–12, 48

Marine Helicopter Squadron One (HMX1), 50

V

About the Author

Captain Alexander G. Monroe, USN (Ret.) is an honors graduate of Christchurch School. Thereafter, he matriculated at the University of Virginia, entered the Navy ROTC program, and earned his bachelor of arts degree, "with distinction," in June 1964. Following his commissioning on the twentieth anniversary of D-Day in Normandy, he served as gunnery officer and an underway officer of the deck on USS *Aucilla* (AO-56), homeported in Norfolk, Virginia. Following active duty, he enrolled at The College of William and Mary and concurrently affiliated with the active Navy Reserve. He earned his M.A. in government and was employed as a member of the city manager's staff in Richmond, Virginia, and served as city records manager/archivist. He deployed to the Arabian Gulf in 1988 during the tanker reflagging operation known as Earnest Will, completing a special assignment for the director of naval history. He also served at the U.S. Naval Base at Guantanamo Bay, Cuba, in 1992, during humanitarian care operations involving Haitians. He is the author of official reports on humanitarian care for Haitians who sought parole as asylum seekers at the U.S. Naval Base, Guantanamo Bay, Cuba, and on U.S. Atlantic Command assistance to civilian law enforcement authorities in the "War on Drugs." He has earned the Defense Meritorious Service Medal, the Meritorious Service Medal, and the Navy Commendation Medal in service of the United States. Captain Monroe lives and writes in Richmond, Virginia.